DESPAIR: SICKNESS OR SIN?

HOPELESSNESS AND HEALING IN THE CHRISTIAN LIFE

Mary Louise Bringle

ABINGDON PRESS
Nashville

DESPAIR: SICKNESS OR SIN?
HOPELESSNESS AND HEALING IN THE CHRISTIAN LIFE

Copyright © 1990 by Abingdon Press.

Library of Congress Cataloging-in-Publication Data

Bringle, Mary Louise, 1953–
    Despair: sickness or sin? : hopelessness and healing in the Christian
    life. / Mary Louise Bringle.
        p.   cm.
    Includes bibliographical references
    ISBN 0-687-10493-9 (alk. paper)
    1. Despair—Religious aspects—Christianity. 2. Health—Religious
    aspects—Christianity. 3. Sin. 4. Hope—Religious aspects—Chris-
    tianity. 5. Laziness. I. Title.
BT774.5.B75 1990   233—dc20   90-43488

Excerpts from *Final Payments* by Mary Gordon, ©1978 by Mary Gordon, used by permission of Random House, Inc.

Printed in the United States of America on acid-free paper

CONTENTS

ACKNOWLEDGEMENTS

It is hard to be hopeful alone; it is not good that any of us should have to be so. Despair festers in isolation. It feeds on the sense that we must single-handedly find our way out of the impasse of present circumstances while we feel ourselves utterly unable to see any escape or resolution. Hope, on the other hand, finds its sustenance in community: in the abiding care of persons who bear one another's burdens, listen to one another's sorrows, remind one another of the promises of the future — even when those promises feel most remote. Over the eight years that I have been working on this manuscript, first as a doctoral dissertation and now as a book, numerous people have acted to counter my inclinations to despair and to bolster and replenish my hope.

I suspect that every doctoral dissertation is written, at some point or other, *in* despair, though not every one takes despair as its focal topic. During the research and writing of this work, which seemed so often to be both "in" and "of" despairing, three faculty members at Emory University proved centrally important: Jack Boozer (dissertation director, mentor, father confessor, friend); Don Saliers (multi-talented *Gesprächspartner* extraordinaire); and Jim Fowler (sponsor, faith-full respondent, and now author of the Foreword to this book). Anne Mayeaux and John Fenton played further key roles on my dissertation committee. T. Nease counseled me pastorally and personably throughout the project. Miriam Needham, Louanne Bachner, and William Warren provided invaluable companionship and support.

In the transition from dissertation to book, a few other persons have contributed significantly. David Blumenthal, also at Emory, prodded me into seeking publication. Rex Matthews at Abingdon combined enthusiasm for the project with professional attention to detail and personal wit and warm-heartedness. Edna Ann Loftus at St. Andrews Presbyterian College read drafts of several chapters and shared countless lunches which drew me out of the loneliness of writing. Many other colleagues at St. Andrews have helped in subtle and sustaining ways by creating a community which cares not only about scholarship but also, preeminently, about humaneness.

From beginning to end, three other persons or groups of persons have offered resources which merit explicit acknowledgement. My parents have given me words and care — care about and with words, care in so many other arenas. Shirley Arnold has ministered in daily ways with her steadying presence. Finally, at Emory and most recently at St. Andrews Presbyterian College, a great many students have shared their freshness and eagerness with me, and have brought me joy — which is perhaps (as Gregory the Great and Martin Luther both noted) the greatest antidote to despairing.

In memoriam

Jack S. Boozer

FOREWORD

It is both a pleasure and an honor to join Abingdon Press in introducing the work of one of the outstanding younger theologians emerging on the American scene in the present period. Generative as a teacher of undergraduates, compelling as a contributor to feminist inquiry in the study of religion, here we encounter Mary Louise Bringle as a historical and practical theologian of lucid penetration and graceful construction. In a voice that achieves a consistent blending of personal presence, careful exposition, and sustained argumentation, Bringle offers sure guidance into a set of questions that have striking contemporary and classical relevance.

Despair: Sickness or Sin? is a book likely to prove both timely and timeless. Bringle did not write with an eye to capitalizing upon the current discussions in our society of the many patterns of pain centering on a sense of personal emptiness or lack of self worth. Nonetheless, her astute analysis of despair has profound implications both for understanding and for treating eating disorders, substance abuse, sexual obsessiveness, and various types of withdrawing or compulsive behaviors. These features make hers a timely book in our present context.

On the other hand, Bringle's study traces the history of a discussion regarding the dynamics and etiology of despair which draws on the rich language of psychologies that long antedate the post-Freudian and humanistic psychological categories in which these matters are chiefly discussed today. She makes us

11

recall that *psyche* is the Greek term for *soul*, and that psychology, as the *logos* or reasoned science of the soul, properly deals with the spiritual and faith dimensions of alienation, isolation, and feelings of resigned impotence. In retrieving the thinking of theologians and spiritual interpreters from the third through the twentieth centuries, she offers a timeless contribution to our understanding of a universal dynamic of the soul as interpreted in dialogue with Christian traditions.

Bringle makes no apology for offering both a scholarly book and a book written in dialogue with Christian sources. In the spirit of sharing with others the wealth from a classic tradition, she confidently offers the fruits of years of careful and creative scholarly engagement with Christian theology. At the same time, she demonstrates her conviction that theology, when it does its proper work, stays very close to human experience and suffering. Her work moves primarily in an inductive way, offering rich descriptions of human experiences and the suffering of despair, and then of the means by which those in despair sometimes find and receive healing and restorative strength.

To establish an experiential baseline for her study and dialogue with the reader, Bringle draws from contemporary fiction the stories of two women in despair — Celie in Alice Walker's *The Color Purple*, and Isabel in Mary Gordon's *Final Payments*. In her depiction of these two characters, one African American, the other Anglo American, the author conveys the situational factors that threaten to make the lives of each of the protagonists ones of quiet and isolated despairing. Celie, abused by her alleged father, forcibly separated from her children and from her sister, and sold to a cruel and oppressive "husband," faces the temptation of resignation and suicide. Isabel, spending the best years of her young adulthood in the lonely and totally restrictive task of caring for her invalid father, is suddenly released by his death to the facing of her isolation, her erosion from the fullness of life around her, and the recognition that with his passing her life no longer has any obvious center or purpose at all. Economic in sketching these women's experiences, Bringle nonetheless evokes their situations with faithfulness and full-rounded description. Her account and analysis of the means by which each finds a path toward personal renewal and regrounding in faith provides the basis for identifying the dialectical relation between self-effort and courage, on the one hand, and the power of God's grace — mediated in multiple ways — on the other. Bringle sees this dialectic of effort and grace as essential for bringing about the overcoming of despair and the restoration of will, purpose, energy, and meaning in life.

Bringle finds the two sides of this dialectic represented in essential ways in historic Catholic and Protestant discussions of despair. Though it is a bit anachronistic to view such writers as Evagrius Ponticus (4th century), John Cassian (5th century), and Gregory the Great (7th century) as "Catholic" writers, Bringle demonstrates that they represent the sources in Catholicism of the "seven deadly sins" tradition which has been chiefly preserved by the church of Rome. Bringle shows how despair came to be viewed as one of the daughters of *acedia* (identified by the desert fathers as weakness of distractability and sloth, the "sin of the noonday sun") and *tristitia* (a deep, pervasive sadness bringing pain and virtual paralysis). These came to be combined in the deadly sins tradition into *tristitia*. In a variety of ways these "Catholic" writers — "the old moralists," she calls them — respond to despair as though it is a sin resulting from failure of the will and from the inadequate exercise of discipline.

Bringing forward her accounts of Celie's and Isabel's struggles with despair, Bringle shows how, to a point, their responses to their situations do depend significantly on the resoluteness, the will to struggle and the unwillingness to be defined by their contexts, which they maintained. An essential element in dealing with despair she finds in Thomas Aquinas's retrieval of the Aristotelian tradition of the *virtues*. Especially important is the emphasis on the virtue *fortitudo* (courage) for dealing with despair.

On the other hand, Bringle finds in the Reformation tradition, drawing upon the apostle Paul and Augustine for its inspiration, the approach to despair that constitutes the other pole of the dialectic of healing and restoration. This is the focus on grace and faith. Martin Luther moves to the center here, a man of profound personal experiences of *tristitia* and *Anfechtungen* — the strong German term for the kind of emotional afflictions that erode one's basic sense of worth and undermine one's sense of balance or hope. Luther writes of the grace of God as the essential power by which one can be released from the grips of despair. And while Luther waxes eloquent about the power of the word of God in preaching and in the sacraments as the means of this grace, he also affirms the key roles of friends and human company, music, work, food, humor, and active life and movement to help break the grip of despair. All these, he suggests, are forms grace takes in healing and releasing the man or woman in despair.

The broadly Catholic tradition connects despair with the sins of distractability, isolation, and the lack of courage to face one's situation with the necessary renunciations. It relies upon the sacraments and the penitential system, as well as positive disciplines of prayer and work, to help mediate the grace of forgiveness and reempowerment to deal with the downward spiral of distortions and isolation which despair brings. The broadly Protestant tradition, on the other hand, sees despair as the focal point for the central sin (singular and comprehensive) besetting humankind, that of mistrust of God's love, God's acceptance, and of God's effective providential care for us and for the world. Despair, for Luther — and in an even more radical way for Kierkegaard — involves falling into the bondage of a judgment about oneself that one is worthless, powerless, and hopeless; that this condition must be concealed from others and borne alone; and that this negative, helpless, futureless condition is either seen and ratified by God, or that God is ineffectual as regards any possibility of transforming the valence of despair that negates all worth and meaning for one's life.

Today it is the discussion of *shame* that most directly parallels Bringle's adroit evocation and clarification of despair. Shame is the emotion arising out of a judgment about the self that one is centrally and pervasively lacking, damaged, or unworthy. In shame one is not just embarrassed about a mistake or mistakes one has made. Rather, one feels the deep embarrassment arising from the judgment that at one's core one *is* a mistake. In shame one tries to conceal the "real" self, constructs a "false self," and in an impossible contradiction, sets out to take on the heroic task or find the ideal relational connection that will overcome the terrible verdict of one's emptiness and lack of worth. Shame involves despair about the self, despair about the world — no one there could know the *real* me and still love me — and despair about God. Like my friends and relations, God also cannot be trusted to love, accept, heal or strengthen the wretched creature that is me.

Shame and despair have rootage in our relations, and in the contexts and events of our lives. They are, as Bringle correctly indicates, patterns of *construal* of our selves in relation to others, the world and God. Grace, in its many forms, is the only antidote to despair and to the shame that most often underlies it. One of the most wonderful features of Bringle's book is its subtle but powerfully persuasive depiction of the multi-leveled dynamics of grace making possible the recovery of courage, the restoration to community and relationship, and the bringing of one's condition of despair into the sunlight of the unconditional love of friend, of lover and community, and of a loving God.

This is a book of uncommon depth and wisdom. Never didactic, it offers a new grammar of grace, a new vernacular of practical redemption from the self-absorption of despair and shame. A passionate love suffuses this writing — a love of God and of human beings — founded on a convictional hope for the healing of all of us who are subject to the isolating bondage of despair. Read, savor, and learn.

James W. Fowler
Emory University

INTRODUCTION

The Question: Sickness or Sin?

It shows a deep knowledge of human nature that the old moralists should have included *tristitia* among the *septem vitia principalis*.
That is what my father called *a silent despair*.

Søren Kierkegaard, Journals

These sentences hit me between the eyes the first time I read them. They still affect me profoundly, disturbingly. At the time I was taking a graduate seminar on Kierkegaard, reading in his journals and struggling through the densities of *The Sickness Unto Death*, his intricate analysis of the phenomenon of despair. In the light of Kierkegaard's writings, I looked at the world around me: a world in which suicide had become the single largest cause of death among teenagers; a world in which homelessness and starvation coexisted with indecent affluence; a world in which terrorist activity had become commonplace and the tensions of racial, ethnic, and religious violence threatened to erupt in large-scale warfare which might even culminate in nuclear disaster. In such a world, was despair really sinful? It seemed to me, instead, to make rather good sense.

At the opening of his book *Images of Hope*, William Lynch observes that "We are passing through a period of fascination with despair."[1] How could it be otherwise? We are fascinated by despair because we are all touched by it, to one degree or another. In the face of personal frustrations and failures, we

17

struggle to maintain our energies and enthusiasms for living; in the shadow of past disasters and present dilemmas, we struggle to preserve our faith and hope for the whole human future. The words of Henry David Thoreau, written over a hundred years ago, sound strikingly contemporary: "The mass of men [and women] lead lives of quiet desperation."[2]

"Quiet desperation"; "a silent despair." In pondering the frequency of such phenomena, I found myself wondering: What reason did the "old moralists" have for including *desperatio* among the seven principal sins? At the very least, such inclusion sounded singularly unpastoral:

"Reverend, I've been in despair lately."
"Repent, you sinner!"

That scenario seemed to rank in bad clerical advice right up with telling a battered woman to go home and submit to her husband. I was tempted to discount the designation of despair as sinful, to consider it something belonging to a harsher, less psychologically sophisticated era.

And yet . . . something about that label stuck in my mind. I began to remember another phrase from the Christian tradition which had similarly troubled me — the command in I Thessalonians to "Rejoice always, pray constantly, and give thanks in all things" (I Thess. 5:16–18). This call to constant rejoicing clearly fit with Kierkegaard's condemnation of despair. Indeed, I thought: if the Christian life is supposed to be animated by steady joy and blessed assurance in the providence of God, then perhaps the sadness of despair — at least sometimes — is out of place.

But when? I recalled a conversation I had had with a young woman, a student in one of my classes, who told me how a friend of hers had been drummed out of their church youth fellowship because he had been depressed — which had prompted their youth leader to question the authenticity of his "Christian conversion." I cringed. Garish images swarmed into mind: images of sugar-coated Christians smiling placidly — if not vapidly — through the trials of life. Surely this was not what Paul or Kierkegaard or the "old moralists" had intended!

I was presented with a dilemma of both theological and deeply personal importance. On the one hand, Christian tradition did mandate that the theological virtues were faith, hope, and love. Despair seemed clearly to involve a renunciation of hope (and, to a lesser degree, of the other two). Yet, on the other hand, despair did not seem to me to be something for which a person could fairly — or pastorally — be held accountable. Could I help it that sometimes I fell into despair upon contemplating the world's problems or my own life situation? Could the "inauthentically converted" college student — and the unprecedented numbers of young people like him who finally turned to suicide for an escape — help their depression? Was despair not something more akin to an illness, induced by sometimes inescapable circumstances, calling for sympathy, therapy, and healing? Had the "old moralists" really been so astute in classifying it among the seven principal vices? Was despair a sickness or a sin?

The pages that follow are an attempt to wrestle with that question, to determine what contemporary relevance — if any — may lie in the old moralists' theological analysis. What sense did it make for them, what sense might it make for us, to consider despair as sinful? How would such consideration re-cast our images of sin and of virtue? How would it re-shape the contours of our Christian life together?

Before embarking upon an exploration of these questions, two prefatory comments need to be made. The first has to do with the preceding allusion to our "Christian" life together. What follows is unapologetically a work of Christian theology, both in its historical analysis and its contemporary constructions. I am clearly writing from a confessional perspective. My aim is not to persuade those whose life-orientations lie outside Christianity of the exclusive validity of the Christian analysis. Rather, my aim is to work within the presuppositions of the Christian tradition — its doctrines, symbols, and stories — in an effort to draw out their implications for a fruitful interpretation of human experience. The test question for the analysis which follows, thus, is *not* "Is it objectively true?" but rather "Does it help me to make sense of the way I live my life as an individual and as a participant within a particular faith community?"

The second prefatory comment has to do with the central term under discussion in this exploration: the term *despair*. I do not intend at this juncture to provide an exact definition for it. Rather, my intent is to let such a definition emerge through the following chapters. Proceeding inductively, moving from particulars to generalities, these chapters offer an amalgam of descriptions through which the reader is invited to shape a composite definition. Such an approach resembles the method we might use to teach the meaning of "despair" to a person whose English vocabulary was limited and whose native language we did not know: experiential illustrations are worth thousands of dictionary-definition words.

Still, without violating the inductive manner of proceeding, one word of elucidation needs to be stated. I do wish to explore the phenomenon of despair expansively, in its rich range of manifestations. Nevertheless, I also intend to use the term precisely, holding it close to its etymological meaning: *desperatio*, the absence (*de*) of hope (*spes*). Thus, "despair" is not simply a loose equivalent for a term like "depression" or "despondency." Rather, it names one particular dimension of such wider depressive affects — the dimension having to do with future-orientation. Despair inheres in the conclusion (valid or invalid, but nonetheless painful) that our yearnings — for ourselves or our wider communities — will never be fulfilled.

The following chapters show us this experience of poignant yearning in a variety of guises. Chapter One looks at two recent novels which describe a character's journey through despair. Chapter Two examines the writings of a variety of "Church Fathers" [*sic*] — the "old moralists" among them — in order to discern precisely what they were targeting when they included despair among the principal vices. Chapter Three turns to Kierkegaard's nineteenth century analysis, looking head-on at his reasons for classifying despair as "the sickness unto death" and, indeed, as the very epitome of sin. Chapters Four and Five return to contemporary experience. The former of these wrestles with the theoretically and personally troubling matter of volition: Can we be held accountable for our despairing? The latter broaches the theological and pastoral questions: What do we, as Christians, have distinctively and helpfully to say to the person who is despairing; and conversely, what does the experience of despair have to say to us about our convictions and responsibilities as members of the Christian family?

A final word before embarking. What follows is an academic study, calling upon a wide range of resources in literature, church history, phenomenological and theological analysis. But it is not simply an exercise in academia. For me, and I suspect for anyone reading this book, despair is an intensely personal issue. It tears at our hearts and eats away at the resources which sustain our ability to find life worth living. To despair is to wish we could simply *not be*, because being seems bereft of promise, hope, vitality, and meaning. "Quiet desperation" fills our days with dullness and our nights with silent weeping. To study such experiences is not to abstract from them into the realms of rarefied theory. Rather, it is to enter into them in an effort to gain clarity and to replenish our courage. To despair is to be human and vulnerable to the pains of facing into an uncertain future. To study despair is to share our vulnerability — and in sharing, to find communal resources which offer us consolation, healing, and hope for our journeys. Let us, then, begin.

CHAPTER 1

The Contemporary Experience: Isabel's and Celie's Stories

Isabel's father has just died, leaving her alone in the world with no sense of direction or identity or meaning. Celie's sister has disappeared, leaving her aching for someone to love who will love her in return, leaving her bereft of a sense of connectedness and of value. Both women are in despair.

On the outside, the two characters could scarcely be more different. Isabel, from Mary Gordon's novel *Final Payments*, is a New Yorker, a lapsed Irish Catholic, a beauty (so she is told), well-educated, situated with relative comfort in a middle class world. Celie, from Alice Walker's *The Color Purple*, is a Southern black woman, "ugly" (by other peoples' and her own harsh estimations), implicitly religious, deprived of the opportunity to pursue an education, deprived of many of life's basic amenities. Their stories are very different in setting and circumstance and surface details. Yet, on the inside, at a deep level, both stories exemplify a common struggle: a struggle with love and loss, with hope and hopelessness, with the monstrousness of life and the challenge to affirm it despite its monstrosity.

Because of the diversity of their stories and the commonality of their quest, Isabel and Celie serve as fruitful models for a study of despair. Their lives, both of them narrated in the first person, give voice to a series of pertinent and provocative issues. When and why does a person fall into despair — from what causes or occasions: rational or irrational, escapable or inescapable, just or unjust? What does despair feel like: how does it look, act, smell, taste, and sound? What difference does it make if despair is experienced and explicated in a spiritual, as opposed to a strictly secular, context? What sources and resources offer healing for the person in despair?

Isabel's and Celie's stories speak to these questions in markedly similar ways. They make for moving reading and re-reading in their own right. What is more, for the purposes of the present study, they offer an imagistic and invaluable entry into exploring whether despair is ultimately more sickness or sin.

Causes and Occasions of Despairing

Both Isabel and Celie experience their despair in waves — from an initial loss or deprivation, to a preliminary recovery, to a more acute sense of lostness, to a culminating struggle for spiritual as well as emotional and physical resolution.

Isabel

Isabel's father has just died. The novel *Final Payments* opens with its narrator-protagonist strangely dry-eyed on the day of his funeral. In light of her seeming calm, Isabel cautions: "Do not think that . . . I attach to my father's existence less than a murderous importance" (9).[1] Her words are carefully, brutally chosen. For the past eleven years, since the age of nineteen, she has devoted herself exclusively to caring for her father. "I gave up my life for him," she says, and it is true (9). She has given up friendships, profession, pleasures, all but the most tenuous and functional of connections with the world outside her home. Her mother dead since Isabel's infancy, her father increasingly enfeebled by a series of strokes, she centers her life around the hospital bed positioned prominently on the ground floor of the house. Helping her father into bed and out of bed, attending to his bodily functions, bathing him, feeding him, sitting with him for hours on end while she reads to herself or to him and he scratches her head — thus her days are consumed. "Care of an invalid has this great virtue," she acknowledges: "one never has to wonder what there is to do. Life is simple and inevitable and straightforward. . . . My life had the balletic attraction of routine" (11).

Her father's death ruptures that routine. From a rhythmic certainty which had held her "encased in meaning like crystal," (12) Isabel erupts into a radical uncertainty in which she no longer knows who she is or how to fill her time. "I felt . . . light as a spaceman in a gravityless universe," she writes (14); the weight of a fixed identity and a fixed schedule no longer holds her securely to the ground. A few days after the funeral, Isabel goes out with a woman friend from high school, her first such outing in years. Her friend suggests that Isabel spend the night. "It suddenly occurred to me that I had no one to ask permission of, no one to report back to. I felt myself looking down at my life from a height, in a thin layer of ozone where nothing bred" (48). Isabel's new aloneness and purposelessness leave her feeling dizzy and barren and scared.

From this first wave of grief and despair, however, Isabel makes a preliminary and partial recovery. With the help of her two remaining parochial school friends, she finds a job and she meets a lover. Life begins to look meaningful again, but it is not a meaningfulness devoid of ambiguity. Hugh, her lover, is married — seriously estranged from his wife, yet strongly devoted to his children. Isabel lucidly recognizes the pain she courts in such a situation. At the end of a luncheon encounter early in the relationship, she observes:

> He walked away. The sight of his back was so beautiful that I felt a kind of despair. If he wanted me, my life would be full of separations. He would always be going away, back to his children, to his wife (140).

To love, particularly to love in this context of multiple and ambiguous commitments, reopens the potentiality for loss and grieving. "If I let Hugh love me like that," she realizes, "if I said to life,'This is what I want, only this; I can make do with nothing else,' then I was immensely vulnerable" (190).

Eventually, foreseeably, that vulnerability comes crashing down around her. An excruciating confrontation with Hugh's wife forces her to cut off the relationship which had become her new central link in finding life worth living. The separation from Hugh accentuates the separation from her father. Pain which had not been fully plumbed in the first wave of loss, in this second wave completely engulfs her. As she sits reeling from the wife's accusations, the thoughts that press into consciousness are of the earlier, not the later, separation. "It came to me, with perfect clarity, that my father was dead; he was not with me; I would never see him again" (199). Tears unshed on the day of the funeral finally erupt: "And then it broke, the terror. . . . I wept like an animal. My mouth was open. I rocked and rocked. . . . 'I want to die. I only want to die,' I kept saying" (199). The present is achingly empty; the future holds no promise. Death alone seems to offer the solace of an escape from hurting. Isabel has lost the two loves of her life and, with them, the sure sense of her own purpose and identity. She sinks into despair.

Celie

Like Isabel in *Final Payments*, Celie in *The Color Purple* suffers waves of loss and deprivation which cumulatively plunge her into despair. Only fourteen when the novel opens, Celie's tragic experiences have aged her physically and emotionally beyond Isabel's thirty-year-old fragility. The early death of Isabel's mother left her in the close if constricting circle of her father's affections. The untimely death of Celie's mother leaves her victim to her (alleged) father's sexual assaults. He gets her pregnant twice; he tears her babies away from her in the night — to kill them in the woods, she imagines, or to sell them. The pains to her, body and spirit, are anguishing.

Everything in Celie's circumstances serves to deplete her self-esteem. Her mother dies, raging at her in unreasoned fury. Her father tells her she is ugly and evil. Lest other people believe any accounts of his assaults on her, he insists that she tells lies. Although she loves school, at the first sign of her pregnancy he yanks her out, telling her she is too stupid to learn. Verbal and physical abuse pile on top of each other. Her father rapes her and beats her and, with no more concern than for a property transaction, he gives her in marriage to another man who will continue to treat her just the same.

The one thing in Celie's circumstances which does not rob her of self-esteem is the relationship with her sister. Nettie tells her she is smart. Nettie teaches and loves and encourages her, exhorting her that she must learn how to fight. But Celie knows implicitly that, in her circumstances, fighting is dangerous. In her circumstances, it is the best that she can do simply to survive. Even her barest efforts at survival are threatened when Celie's husband "Mr.____," angry that Nettie rebuffs his sexual overtures, forces her to leave his premises. She promises Celie to write, but no letters come. Having lost her only source of comfort, Celie decides to stop feeling altogether. Most of all, she deadens her anger. Even when Mr.____ beats her, she remains numb. She imagines herself wooden, a tree. Anaesthesia becomes preferable to heart-heaviness, loneliness, and rage.

Like Isabel, Celie makes an initial emergence from despair through a significant love relationship. Isabel fell in love with a married man; Celie falls in love with a woman who is romantically and sexually involved with Celie's own husband. The irrepressible Shug Avery, woman-about-town and blues singer extraordinaire, comes to stay with Mr.____ while she recovers from a venereal disease. Celie nurses her, feeling no jealousy at having a rival for her husband's affections in the house. In fact, given the brutality of her relationship with Mr.____, the diversion of his attentions comes as a relief.

Celie's jealousy, however, is awakened by the intensity of the passion that she comes to feel for Shug, and by the fear that such passion cannot be returned. When Shug sings in public, Celie is painfully aware that both she and her husband look on with admiration. Yet she is sure that Shug will return only Mr.____'s affections. Having opened herself to feel again, Celie finds this anticipation of rejection to be devastating. Women love men, not other women, she tells herself. Even though that is how life is "'sposed" to be, the realization tugs heavily at her heart.

The miracle is that Celie is not rejected. Shug lavishes exuberance and tenderness and sensuality upon her. She protects her and elicits her confidences. Celie tells her all the griefs of her mother's death, her sister's departure, her husband's brutality, and her utter lovelessness. Shug counters with the amazing affirmation: "But I love you, Miss Celie" (109).

In the fullness of that affirmation, Celie flowers. Simply sitting in Shug's presence, for once in her life, she is able to feel good about herself. Even after weathering painful revelations about her family and about Mr.____'s meanness in hiding her sister's letters, she emerges with the resilience to declare: "I'm pore, I'm black, I may be ugly and can't cook. . . . But I'm here." To which Shug answers, resoundingly, "Amen" (187).

But despair comes in waves. After the calm of a preliminary recovery comes the crashing devastation of new loss. As Isabel feels forced to leave Hugh, so Shug feels compelled to leave Celie in order to have a "last fling" with a younger man. Initially, Celie's protective numbness returns. But through Shug, she has learned to feel so much that the anaesthesia wears off dreadfully quickly. Her heart aches. The future loses its luster. "Being alive begin to seem like an awful strain" (225). Thus, Celie arrives at the same still point to which grief and separation brought Isabel. Life no longer seems worth living, out of the depths of her despair.

Summary

Final Payments and *The Color Purple* provide vivid depictions of the events — both environmental and psychological — through which their major characters move from hope to despair, from meaning to a confrontation with meaninglessness. For Isabel and Celie, different though they are, the occasions provocative of despair show remarkable parallels. Both women suffer from an initially weak sense of self, induced by various environmental deprivations and, particularly in Celie's case, exacerbated by the oppressions of a racist and sexist society. Both yearn intensely for connectedness, for a relationship which will confer and confirm their value and give them the strength to continue combatting the situations surrounding them. Out of their yearning, they pin all their emotional hopes onto one inaccessible other. When relationship with this other falters, they reel from the losses which not only plunge them into isolation, but which also threaten their newly acquired and still shaky self-affirmation. They want and need more from a single, worldly relationship than it can sustain. When the fragile foundations fall out from under their sense of meaning, both women lose the energy and imagination to see beyond their immediate pain; the bitterness of the past and the barrenness of the present combine to provoke a foreclosure on the future. In skeletal form, these are the common causes and occasions of Isabel's and Celie's despair. Future explorations will show just how common — how universal, indeed — such provocations to despairing can be.

The Feel of Despair

Not only do Mary Gordon and Alice Walker provide an *etiology* of despair in *Final Payments* and *The Color Purple*; they also present a *phenomenology*. That is to say, in addition to chronicling the causes of despair, they further attend to its multiple experiential dimensions. With extraordinary attention to detail, they evoke the comprehensive "feel" of despair — how it looks, acts, sounds, smells, tastes; how it comes to experience and to expression. This evocation plays a crucial role in shaping an emergent, imagistic definition of the phenomenon, laying the groundwork for a more systematic exploration of despair as sin or sickness in chapters to come.

Isabel

What does despair feel like? What in the experience of despairing sets it apart from other emotions and dispositions — from grief or disappointment, from anger or more general depression? There is no better way to begin tackling these distinctions than to look closely at the phenomenon as it presents itself to lived human experience. Mary Gordon's portrayal of Isabel, though fictional, rings with the kind of authenticity that makes it a rich resource for such scrutiny.

If despair had a color, it would be shades of gray. "I thought of my life now," Isabel writes: "austere, a lunar color, whites and grays, the temperature of the moon" (108). It is not the moon of poets and lovers to which she refers, however — not a shining silver orb or slender sickle. It is, rather, a cratered, pock-marked, forbidding surface — arid, where no earth creature can long survive. Elsewhere, Isabel had felt herself "looking down

29

at [her] life from a height, in a thin layer of ozone where nothing bred" (48). This is the dwelling place of her despair — the dark side of the moon: secretive, sterile, chill. Surely it is more than coincidence that the ancient Greek humoral psychologists linked despair to melancholia, an excess of black bile, a predominance of the cold, dry humor.

As the shades of gray range from pallid to inky, so the feel of despair ranges from apathy to anguish. "As with each new stroke [my father] was able to do less for himself," Isabel explains, "the days were filled, and I grew dull" (11). No end to his suffering, or to her self-sacrifice, appears in sight. This is a pale, early stage of her despairing. After her father's death, after separation from her lover finally forces her to acknowledge loneliness and loss and mortality, her apathy becomes even more pronounced. It becomes a thick, protective covering. "You could do anything if you gave up thinking that it mattered what you did," she sighs, "if you gave up caring for one thing more than any other" (213).

Yet this protection does not always hold; sometimes hurt can force its way into conscious recognition:

> My father was dead. I knew what that meant now. I was entirely unsafe, entirely alone. Now pain was all around me; I was drowning in pain (198).

Isabel sinks under waves of anguish, her body wracked with uncontrollable weeping:

> . . . I rolled around, back and forth, from one side of my body to the other, as if the motion would make the pain stop (199).

The terror of utter hopelessness seizes her, "that buzzing pain, black, purple, at the back of my skull" (203). Isabel finds herself plunged into the night with no morning, the deepest pitch in the coloration and tonality of despair.

Like this alternation between apathy and anguish, despair in Isabel's experience also manifests an alternation between entrapment and dizzying expanse. One moment, she succumbs to the torpor born out of a sense of inevitability; the future appears as a bleak sameness, bearing no promise of relief or of novelty. The next moment, however, a threat of perpetual

THE CONTEMPORARY EXPERIENCE

novelty induces terror; the moorings no longer hold, the potential for meaning and security drifts on an uncertain sea. Isabel gives voice to this very alternation. Alone in an empty house on the day after the funeral, surrounded by newly-useless sickroom paraphernalia, she laments: "What I had was either too much, things that would smother me, or nothing at all, nothing to break my fall" (38).

The feeling of too much, of accumulation, of "the pileup of things and days and lives" proves overwhelming (38). The sight of old broccoli "liquefying" in the unattended vegetable bin of the refrigerator reduces her to tears (40). Later, the confrontation with Hugh's wife has a similar impact. Isabel had summoned some resistance; she had begun an escape from her entrapment. "But," she confesses, "that was before it happened":

> *It: it* meant that woman pointing her finger, knowing in my body that my father was dead, that I would never see him again, that I was not a good person. I lay down in the bed I had just got out of. My nightgown was beginning to smell fishy but I was too tired to change it (208).

Everything tires her. Her activities reduce themselves to eating and sleeping. She grows fat — a heaviness of body to match her heaviness of spirit. But her appearance no longer matters. "This seemed as inevitable as the color of my hair," Isabel confides. "I would eat foods quickly, furtively, in this dark room. Then I would sleep here" (222). To eat, to sleep, to escape — it is a slow suicide she chooses. The trap of despair closes off all other options.

Yet, at other moments, it is not the closure, but the vast openness of options that assaults her. In contrast to "accumulation" hovers a "vague agoraphobia," a "great airiness" of feeling (38). Isabel keeps looking down at her life from a height. What she sees is its indeterminacy: if she is not the good-daughter-caring-for-her-invalid-father, who is she? A childhood memory supplies her with an answering image. She recalls a picture book about career choices. On the first page was a picture of a little girl, with a circular hole where her head should be. Turning the pages filled the hole with the faces and headgear

31

of different career possibilities. "It reminded me of myself," Isabel observes: "the perfectly empty circle of the child's head and the sickening expanse of potential" (59). Too little certainty is as bad as too much certainty. Agoraphobia or claustrophobia, airiness or suffocation — either extreme can body forth despair.

One final feature of Isabel's despair deserves to be mentioned. Not only does it make her feel alternately anguished or apathetic, dull or dizzy; it also leaves her feeling cut off from the rest of the world. At first, this is an involuntary isolation: "I was radically alone, and my sense of solitariness made me stupid" (193); "People walked around me, but I had no connection with them" (198). But as the feeling of despair intensifies, such isolation becomes something she seeks. "I wished they would not come near me," she says of her friends (202); "If people would just leave me alone" (208). Carrying on a conversation, keeping up a correspondence, requires too much effort. Why bother to speak, if no one else can ever really understand; why bother to care, if caring only heightens vulnerability? . . . How, then, does despair come to experience and to expression? At first, perhaps, by moans and outcries of pain. But ultimately, by a stultifying silence.

Celie

Celie's experience of despair is palpably parallel to Isabel's. She, too, finds herself speechless at the furthest reaches of her desperation. When Shug announces that she is leaving Celie for a younger man, the bitterest betrayal, no words come in reply. The readiest escape from anguish seems to be verbal, as well as emotional, retreat. All she can bring herself to do is to pen monosyllabic responses on small scraps of paper: "Shut up"; "He's a man"; "Spare me" (220). To open lines of communication would be to open avenues for hurting. What is the use?

Similar in its anesthetic silence, Celie's despair is also similar to Isabel's in its alternation between apathy and acute pain. Shug's moment of betrayal presents the clearest case in point. Self-protective apathy is Celie's initial reaction; but then, the pounding of her own heartbeat shatters the defensive stillness, reminding her that she is alive and in pain. Shug, the source of her loving and her new life affirmation, has decided to leave her for someone younger and "cuter." Aging and ugliness wash over her in despairing waves.

The feel of Celie's despair, like Isabel's, shades to listlessness. At the deepest moments of it, she finds that all she can do is sleep. Even suicide becomes a temptation. Short of that final alternative, resignation seems safest: trying to learn not to want anything, ever again.

The biggest difference between Isabel's and Celie's experiences of despair lies in what Mary Gordon's protagonist felt as the alternation between entrapment and a "sickening expanse of potential." Alice Walker's Celie knows well the first side of this dialectic. However, as a poor black woman in a classist, racist, and sexist society, her circumstances are so heavy with necessity that the despair of too much potentiality never enters into her experience. Sister Nettie early on provides the appropriate image. Seeing Celie crushed under the weight of paternal rape, married to a man who abuses her, forced to tend to his house and to care for his hostile children, Nettie says it is as if Celie were buried alive.

Indeed, Celie *is* buried, hard-pressed not so much under "the pileup of things and days and lives" as under their absence — under the deprivation of any things, any days, any life she might truly call her own. Where Isabel saw despair as a color, the dismal gray of the moon, Celie sees it as a stark earth-shape. Even though Nettie had tried to teach her that the world was round, Celie remained skeptical: "I never told her," she said, "how flat it look to me" (20).

Summary

Here, then, is an incipient phenomenology of despair, a descriptive account to disclose the distinctive contours of the experience. Despair feels flat, dim, chill, and lonely; it smells faintly stale; it has no more taste than the white of an egg. The person in despair aches — sometimes dully, sometimes acutely — for a love which is lost, for a meaning gone sour, for an assurance of worth beneath the steady erosion of self-esteem. The feeling-tone of despair differs markedly from the searing red heat of anger. Compared to the surface sting of disappointment, despair is a deep and unremitting stab, reaming out a hollow wound at the very core of being. In affect and sensation, despair and depression are close kin: both have their apathy and anguish, their free-floating dread and their leaden futility. The difference between these two lies in the specificity of their thought-content. Depression is the broader, more all-inclusive term. Despair is the specific surrender of hope for a less barren and more promising future: Isabel sees no promise in a world without Hugh, without her father, without the comforting sureness of her identity as devoted daughter and irreproachably "good person"; Celie sees no promise in a world without Nettie, without Shug, without the whole-making presence of persons whom she loves and who love her in return. Despair haunts them both, in its distinctive and dispiriting guise.

But, you may say, all this is imagery — narrative, poetic depiction. The use of such imagery at this juncture is intentional. The purpose of starting with Isabel's and Celie's stories is to let a definition, however imprecise, emerge out of the living matrix of their experiences. More precision can come later, in chapters of systematic phenomenological and theological analysis. For the present, it is sufficient if Celie's and Isabel's stories have touched off a resonance of sympathy and kindred feeling. It is sufficient if a single descriptive phrase has evoked a response of, "Yes. I, too, have felt that; I, too, know palpably what it means to despair."

Despair and the Spirit

The adjective "dispiriting," above, was deliberately chosen. At its depth, despair is not simply a mental or emotional or bodily affliction; it is an offense against the spirit. This is an insight which Mary Gordon and Alice Walker share, a commonality which further contributes to the suitability of their two novels for an analysis of despair within an ultimately theological context. What difference does it make if despair is experienced in a spiritual, as opposed to a strictly secular, setting? What insights does spirituality lend to an understanding of despair and to an appreciation for the nature of its healing? Once again, Isabel's and Celie's stories prove instructive.

Isabel

At the beginning of *Final Payments*, Isabel is a lapsed Roman Catholic. That detail is significant in her journey: significant, in part, because the father whose death plunges her into despair is the epitome of stringent orthodoxy; significant, in even greater degree, because the events which eventually release her from despair pivot upon an encounter with a priest and a passage of Christian scripture.

Early in her story, Isabel confesses straightforwardly, "I had ceased to believe" (21). Her loss of faith comes gradually; the rituals of the church simply lose their meaning for her, and so she ceases to observe them. Later in the story, however, after separating from Hugh and attempting to make a clean start in her life, she does venture a return to confession. The experience is less than spiritually fulfilling. "I knelt at the altar and said the prayers that the priest had told me to say," she admits: "But I said them to no one; I could not believe that anyone was interested in what I was saying" (226).

Despite her explicit disenchantment with the church and disavowal of belief in God, Isabel's life is implicitly shaped by the Roman Catholicism of her upbringing. It is from the Church that she derives her understanding of what is required to be a "good person." Her devotion to her ailing father wins her this appellation, and it is one which she cherishes, all secular sophistication notwithstanding. She wants the priests, the people in the parish, to nod at her and call her "good." She wants to be thought capable of performing a "pure act of love." She is suspicious of "particular friendships" and is leery of bodily pleasures which might divert her from purity and expose her to reproach.

Yet, underneath this desire for the fixed and satisfying identity of "goodness" runs a further motif: the fear of vulnerability. To love a particular human being rather than a generalized humanity is to open oneself to the possibility of loss. Isabel learns this painfully with the death of her father; she is afraid to learn it again with Hugh. Thus, her leaving him is not only — perhaps not even primarily — out of remorse for their

35

adultery; it is also a failure of nerve. Isabel herself comes to this realization:

> I had wanted to give up all I loved so that I would never lose it. I had tried to kill all that brought me pleasure so that I would not be susceptible. Why had I done it? For safety, certainty, and for the priests, the faceless priests . . . (244).

But pleasing the priests and courting invulnerability prove to be insufficient motivations for Isabel's continued living; in the midst of her despair, she begins to discover that she is longing for something more. Interestingly enough, she arrives at this discovery on the heels of a conversation with a priest, but not with one of the "faceless" variety. Father Mulcahy has been her and her father's confessor for years; he has also been her confidant and friend. When he sees her at the lowest pitch of her despair, when she has let go of her appearance out of a mixture of high-mindedness and apathy and the inanimate yearning to do nothing but eat and sleep, he lovingly admonishes her:

> ". . . watch your weight, honey. God gave you beauty. If you waste it, that's a sin against the fifth commandment."
> "Thou shalt not kill? What does that have to do with it?"
> "It means slow deaths, too," he said (242).

Indeed, a "slow death" is what Isabel has been seeking. Her despair makes life seem too painful, shorn of promise; her fear of loss aggravates the situation. She has attempted a program of self-denial — denying the flesh and its pleasures, denying particular affections — in a misdirected kind of spiritual suicide. Her healing comes in a flash of epiphany, with the recollection of scriptural story — the legacy of her Catholic childhood. It is the story known traditionally as the "anointing at Bethany." On his way toward Jerusalem for the Passover, Jesus stops in Bethany at the house of Mary, Martha, and Lazarus. Mary opens a jar of costly spikenard to anoint Jesus' feet; she then kneels and wipes them with her hair. Judas rebukes her, righteously protesting that the ointment could have been sold to raise money for the poor. Jesus replies: "Let her alone . . . The poor you always have with you, but you do not always have me" (John 12:7–8).

The remarkable words of Isabel's epiphany deserve to be quoted in detail:

> . . . until that moment, climbing the dark stairs . . . to my ugly room, it was a passage I had not understood. It seemed to justify to me the excesses of centuries of fat, tyrannical bankers. But now I understood. What Christ was saying, what he meant, was that the pleasures of that hair, that ointment, must be taken. Because the accidents of death would deprive us soon enough. We must not deprive ourselves, our loved ones, of the luxury of our extravagant affections. We must not try to second-guess death by refusing to love the ones we loved in favor of the anonymous poor.
>
> And it came to me, fumbling in the hallway for the light, that I had been a thief. Like Judas, I had wanted to hide gold, to count it in the dead of night, to parlay it into some safe and murderous investment. It was [safety] . . . I wanted. . . . So that never again would I be found weeping, like Mary, at the tombstone at the break of dawn (243).

Isabel here realizes the extent to which her own despair has been an offense against the spirit. In seeking security, in renouncing the risks of her "extravagant affections," she has robbed life itself of the very energy — the eros — which creates its vitality. Her despair has been absolutizing and presumptuous: it has found the entire future to be drab and meaningless simply because certain elements within it do culminate in death. In a profound theological insight, Isabel recognizes that her delighted pleasure-seeking has been finally less sinful than her despairing self-denial. She comes to understand that she must learn anew to dance while the bridegroom is present, even knowing that one day he will die and she will be left to weep at his tomb. For it is the dancing that renders a life "spirited," spirit-filled. Ultimately, Isabel discovers, it is "spirit" which offers her despair the possibility for genuine solace and healing.

Celie

Celie, too, discovers an important and ultimately healing link between despair and her spirituality. Where Isabel was disenchanted with religion at the outset of her story, Celie begins her narration with an implicit, if unexamined, religious faith. The first line of *The Color Purple* carries the admonition that she must tell no one about her sufferings, except God. Taking those words to heart, Celie puts the first two-thirds of her narration into the form of letters to God. As long as she can at least believe that God is listening to her, she does not feel quite so alone.Given the loneliess of Celie's existence otherwise, that affirmation is a signally important one. Even if her babies are taken from her, even if her sister Nettie is forced to run away, someone remains with her. Even when she is physically and sexually abused, she does not bear the pain completely alone. She can confide in "Old Maker" and receive some comfort from the fact that the trials of this life are passing, but "Heaven last all ways" (47).

That message of comfort, though, is not sufficiently solid to withstand all the adversity which Celie ultimately faces. After a series of tragedies and pages of outpourings to God in His [sic] Heaven which meet with no discernible reply, she finally concludes bitterly, "You must be sleep" (163). She stops writing to God, deciding that if such a being does exist, He [sic] must be as unconcerned with her experience as every other man she has ever known. Still, her denunciation of God intensifies rather than alleviates her despair. "Even if you know he ain't there," she sighs, "trying to do without him is a strain" (176). To lose God, even one who seems deaf and uncaring, is to lose a familiar refuge in times of trouble.

The epiphany which begins to release Celie from the depths of this spiritual despair is remarkably similar in content to Isabel's. Celie's comes, however, not from a priest and a passage of scripture, but from the High Priestess of unorthodoxy, Shug Avery. Shug begins by persuading Celie that the God whose deafness she denounces is not the real God, but simply the one that white people have read into their Bibles. Why else, Shug asks, would He [sic] bear such an uncanny resemblance to a white man?

The God Shug professes instead is neither He nor She, but It: something inside everything and everybody, a special but inseparable part that links each individual being to the greater whole. Shug's own journey away from the white patriarchal God began in an experience of ecstatic union with nature: with trees, with everything living. Celie's first step, under Shug's tutelage, is to realize that the place to seek God is not in a church or holy book — particularly not the church or holy book of a group of oppressors — but inside herself, in her precious connectedness to all of being.

After debunking the churchly image of God as an old white man, the second step in Celie's spiritual epiphany is to realize that God endorses pleasure. "God love all them feelings," Shug declares — even, perhaps especially, sexual feelings. "That's some of the best stuff God did" (178). In wind and wildflowers and the color purple in a field, God is perpetually creating and delighting in beauty. The very least we can do is to share in this divine delight. Admire it; dance with it; anoint it with costly ointments. In Shug's words: "Go with everything that's going, and praise God by liking what you like" (178).

To Celie's feelings of loneliness and unloveliness, Shug's teachings come as a message of salvation by grace. Her despair over an absent or uncaring God is slowly but steadily supplanted by delight in a God who is joyously present throughout the creation. Her despair over lost relationships — to Nettie, to the tragedies of her past — is tempered by the ecstasy of union with all of being. Her pains over maltreatment at the hands of an unjust society are modified: the magnitude of God's creative miracles dwarfs the meanness of any single human being, or even any group of human beings. Perhaps most importantly, her despair of unworthiness — feeling (out of her background of verbal and physical abuse) guilty and ugly and unclean — begins to be washed away. Shug tells her that the love of God does not have to be merited: if God truly loves her for who she is, then she does not have to go to church, or feed the preacher, or act in a sanctified or sanctimonious fashion. The feeling of God's love is a prelude to, not a product of, a life of value. Simply to be the self that one is, enjoying the things one enjoys, is sufficiently lovely in God's eyes. Being triumphs over doing, *is* over ought, and grace over earned worthiness, in this spiritual epiphany which begins to lead Celie out of despair.

Summary

Both Isabel in *Final Payments* and Celie in *The Color Purple* pass through three levels of despair: over the world, over themselves, and over God. Their despair over the world views it as a hostile environment, a source of deprivations and impediments to hope, a place where anything and anyone that one loves is subject to death and decay. Their despair over themselves feels somehow guilty and deserving of the deprivations thrust upon them. They feel not merely wronged, but *wrong* at some deep level of their being: both feel incomplete and unloved, misconstruing this to mean that they are therefore unlovable; both feel shaky in their identities, misconstruing this to mean that their lives are therefore without purpose or value. Finally, their despair over God deprives them of a source which might otherwise confirm value, purpose, and love. Convinced that God is absent, or simply inattentive and uninterested, they both find themselves abandoned and adrift in a cosmos in which there is no guarantee of safe harbor or of certain meaning.

Out of this context of triple despair, however, both Isabel and Celie experience a spiritual awakening which recasts their struggles in a distinctive light. For both women, this awakening involves a penetration beneath surfaces and a probing beyond the confines of present reality. The surface of things looks flat and forbidding to both Isabel and Celie; the present and the immediate future look bleak. To the question, "Is that all there is?," their despair initially answers with door-slamming finality: "Yes, that is all."

But for both women, spirit comes breezing in, tentatively at first, then boldly flinging doors open — spirit substantiated in the words of the Gospel of John or the good news according to Shug Avery. Spirituality teaches both women to relativize the voice of their despair by hearing it within a broader context. Present pains are *not* "all there is"; the deprivations of the immediate moment are not exhaustive of all reality. The body (one's own, or that of a loved one) may be mortal, but it is also very good. While pleasure may be passing, it is nevertheless real and legitimate; having come once, it will — albeit unpredictably — come again. The future does not merely extrapolate from the arid present and past; it can also usher in astonishing novelty. As Celie graphically affirms in a moment of despair which follows her epiphany: "Most times I feels like shit but I felt like shit before in my life and what happen?" (235). She was graced, first by the love of her sister Nettie, and then, astonishingly, by the love of Shug Avery. Who can say what might happen next? Assuredly not the voice of despair, no matter how much false and final-sounding authority it might attempt to arrogate to itself. The ultimate impact of viewing despair within a spiritual context, therefore, is one of relativization and reconfiguration. While despair is, in fact, an offense against the spirit — a depletion of those energies which serve to animate, vitalize, enliven, and "inspirit" human existence — it appears also to be true that some residual element of spirit, not depleted by despair, becomes a countervailing source of revitalization and healing. This residual resource may originate in a gift of personal insight, interpersonal communication, or transpersonal, transcendent benediction. Whatever its ultimate origin, its task is to relativize the claims of despair's foreclosure on the future, and to reconfigure the present in terms of greater depth and richer layers of potentiality and salutary celebration.

Despair and Healing

What, then, heals despair? "Spirit" has already been suggested by way of incipient response: spirit as the source of a dynamic reconstrual of reality which holds out refreshed possibilities for personal worth and ultimate meaning. But this is a partial and an abstract answer at best. To gain greater specificity, one final look at the stories of Isabel and Celie is in order. For in these stories, in the energies which enable these two characters to triumph over despair, lie the seeds of a healing wisdom for anyone who is laboring in a life of "quiet desperation."

Isabel

In the week following Isabel's spiritual epiphany, she sits alone in her room in the evenings and reads the prayers of Holy Week. In the pages of the old Missal which had been given her by her father, she finds a holy card inscribed with a text from the medieval mystic, Dame Julian of Norwich, which reads:

He said not thou shalt not be tempted
He said not thou shalt not be troubled
He said thou shalt not be overcome (244).

The final pages of Isabel's story are the record of how, in fact, having been tempted and troubled, she is nonetheless not overcome by despair. Her victory can be traced to three intricately interwoven threads: to community, to strength, and to sensitive discernment.

Community is a thematic thread which runs throughout the story of *Final Payments*. As Isabel's despair comes in waves, so does her healing from it. In the initial phase of healing after her father's death, Isabel is "rescued" by the community of her old parochial school friends, Liz and Eleanor, who help her to reestablish connections with the world from which she has cut herself off in the years of caring for her invalid parent. These connections take very concrete form. Eleanor helps her to buy new clothes so that she will look less out of date and out of touch. Liz helps her acquire a job and a lover. Isabel moves to a new apartment, where she even finds a bracing thrill in the prospect of arranging for the hook-up of her phone and gas. She confides:

I thought it was exciting to call large companies who would send their men, competent and uniformed, to connect me up to the rest of the world. It made me feel protected and attached to large, benevolent forces (105).

The healing that comes from these connections is real, but temporary; it cannot withstand the pain of the second wave of despair which sweeps over Isabel upon separating from her lover and recognizing afresh the loneliness of living in a world from which her father has been taken in death. To heal that pain requires a community stronger than the functional connections acquired through a new wardrobe and a new telephone line. Isabel begins to find that community in the love offered her by her old confessor and confidant, Father Mulcahy. At the deepest pitch of her loneliness, when she has given up on particular relationships out of her fear of the vulnerability which they induce, he calls and offers to come and visit. The prospect of imminent relief from her isolation moves her to tears:

He would be here in a week, in less than a week. He loved me
so much that he would drive his car ten times the furthest
distance he had driven it. It was a miracle, that love. No one
deserved it; no one could, so I did not have to worry about
deserving it (237).

Feeling this miraculous, this grace-filled love, Isabel begins
to find the strength to make a foray out of despair. Here, traces
of the second thread of healing become visible. Isabel's new
strength, interestingly enough, takes the form of *anger*. Ever
since her father's first illness, and especially since his death, she
has turned her rage at his vulnerability, at life's vulnerability,
inside herself. She has swallowed it — both figuratively, in the
muffled fear of feeling which issues in her apathy and depression; and literally, in the furtive overeating which marks the
fever pitch of her desperation. A crucial step in healing, therefore, comes when she is able to direct her anger outside herself.
Its target is the richly-deserving, sadly despicable Margaret
Casey: Margaret whose sniveling, sniping nature dares to make
insinuations about Father Mulcahy's utterly irreproachable love
for Isabel, attempting to excuse their gross implications by
whining that "He's capable of anything when he's had too much
to drink" (243). At this cheap, unjustifiable attack on a person
she loves for his genuine generosity of spirit, Isabel's fury finally
breaks free. She hurls two glasses onto the floor; she accuses
Margaret of being a "wicked, wicked woman" — which, in fact,
she is. Significantly, it is immediately after this scene that Isabel
experiences her epiphany, "climbing the dark stairs in a rage to
[her] ugly room" (243).

Once Isabel discovers that she has the power to release her
anger, she also discovers the strength to control other aspects
of her life. Swallowing rage had weighted her down with the
burden of her own swelling flesh and with a sense of its inevitability. "I understood . . . that I was fat from eating and sleeping,"
she writes, "But this seemed as inevitable as the color of my
hair" (222). The discovery of inner strength awakens her to the
realization that she is not completely a passive victim. It occurs
to her in a flash: "The body changed, went on changing, and
could be changed. What I had done to myself was not final"
(245). It will take discipline and patience and continued for-

titude, but Isabel realizes that she can take control of her own body, as a metaphor for breaking out of despair's passivity into a degree of control over her own life.

Learning what can and cannot be subjected to such control requires a lesson in discernment, the third thread in the weave of Isabel's healing. Her weight can be controlled; the inevitable death of those she loves cannot be. The challenge is to continue loving nonetheless. Isabel solidifies this lesson of discernment, appropriately, at a Good Friday service which signals her intentional return, after reflection, to the faith of her childhood. "I thought of Christ, of the death of Christ," she says. "We were here to acknowledge the presence of death among us." She continues:

> Everyone I knew and loved would die: Father Mulcahy, Liz, Eleanor. And Hugh. They would be lost to me. I would, one day, never see them again.
> That was what we were kneeling to acknowledge, all of us, on this dark afternoon. We were here to say that we knew about death, we knew about loss, that it would not surprise us. But of course it would surprise us; it had surprised even Christ in the Garden (246).

Death — however sudden, however surprising — remains the one certainty, the one inevitability. Death is the one promise which no one's future ever breaks. But death does not thereby exhaust the future's promises — and therein lies another lesson of discernment to be acquired.

Isabel has been "tempted and troubled" by what Paul Tillich names as the three principal anxieties which threaten "the courage to be," a human being's capacity to affirm life in the face of its negativities: the anxieties of fate and death, of guilt and condemnation, and of emptiness and meaninglessness. She has been panic-stricken by the contingencies of fate and terrified by death's harsh finality. She has felt guilty for not being able to "save" her father, guilty for the pleasures of her body, guilty for being unable to love with pure and impartial disinterest. Emptiness and meaninglessness have engulfed her at the prospect of losing her clear identity as her father's "good" daughter, at the prospect of her life, viewed from dizzying height, as a "sickening expanse of potential." All three of these anxieties meet with healing through the impact of the Good Friday liturgy.

Fate and death, she has already knelt to acknowledge. With that acknowledgement, comes the poignant realization:

> My father was dead; there was the pain. I had loved him, but my love had not been able to help him. Even my love had not made him immune. . . . Love had kept nothing back; not even the smallest disasters. My father had died, but I had not killed him, as I had not been able to save him (246).

There is inappropriate guilt, she learns; but there is also guilt for which remorse is appropriate: a task of discernment, once again. The priests enter the sanctuary and read aloud a litany of human ingratitude and treachery — years of rebellions against the generous constancy of God, rebellions for which the Son of God finally came to die. Yet, even these reproaches come to Isabel as balm: ". . . I had wanted to hear those words spoken," she affirms, ". . . I wanted to hear it in the presence of my kind" (247).

In the presence of her kind, in the gathering assembled for corporate acknowledgement of death and for corporate repentance, Isabel picks back up the thread of community which leads her out of despair to an affirmation of meaning. "For there was death," she concedes; "you had to know that, and betrayal, and the negligence of friends at crucial moments, and their sleep" (247). But that concession does not exhaust Isabel's story. "Christ had been betrayed by His friends," she confesses, in an ownership of appropriate guilt; "but my friends had stood by me in a miracle of love when I had ceased to love them" (247). That miracle of love finally breaks down the barriers erected against it, rushing into the hollows of Isabel's emptiness like life-giving water. The parched expanse of potential which so threatened her with meaninglessness now begins to show shoots of promise.

Isabel telephones her friends and they come to her. Embracing them, she embraces her new discernments about the fragile yet surprisingly resilient ties binding herself to others and to the possibility of meaning. Gone is the illusion of invulnerable loving; gone is the illusion that she can ever again have an identity so certain it will "[encase her] in meaning like crystal" (12). What she has, instead, is the encouraging, the courage-giving opportunity to nurture a new identity, more porous and less imprisoning, in the company of those friends whom she will dare to love, even in the face of vulnerability and unavoidable loss.

At the very end of her story, Isabel gets in the car to drive away with her friends: away from the entrapment of despair toward hope's opening horizon. Her community is staunch, her discernments are hard-won, and her strength is still shaky, but steadily rising. After the apathetic silence into which despair had plunged her, it is apt that she closes the narrative of her healing with the eager affirmation: "There was a great deal I wanted to say" (250). Tempted she has been, and troubled she has been, but it is she who has triumphantly overcome.

Celie

Like Isabel, Celie experiences the temptations and troubles of despair and ultimately emerges triumphant. Celie's triumph of healing can be traced to three threads similar to those woven throughout Isabel's story, although each narrative looms these threads with its own distinctive shadings and frequencies. For Celie, the threads may again be labeled strength, discernment, and community; their colors — like the colors of the room Celie creates for herself at the close of the novel — are red, yellow, and purple.

The bold red thread which weaves in and out of the waves of Celie's emergence from despair is that of strength — the courage to affirm herself despite a brutal background which attempts to rob her of any shred of self-affirmation. This courage comes from a variety of sources. Initially, Celie simply seems born with a survivor's toughness; she may not have the energy to fight, but she knows instinctively how to stay alive. Her sister Nettie augments this strength by complimenting her, exhorting her, teaching her, loving her, treating her like "somebody" when everyone else treats her like an object for abuse. Nettie's forced departure threatens to snuff out any new-found courage, abandoning Celie again to the loneliness of despair.

A new source of encouragement, however, enters Celie's life in the person of Shug Avery. Lusty, flamboyant, and taking flak from nobody, Shug becomes for Celie a model of strength and self-possession. One evening in a nightclub, Shug performs a snatch of music she calls "Miss Celie's song." Celie is amazed at the affirmation that comes from having something named after her. This flush of pride grows deeper as the relationship between the two women deepens. Loving Shug and being loved by Shug, body and soul, increasingly empowers Celie to love herself, to name herself, to take pride in the affirmation: "I am."

Indeed, Celie gains the strength to proclaim her "I am" in the face of the one person who has done the most to destroy this affirmation, her husband Mr.____. Like Isabel, Celie finds fuel for such strength in the release of long pent-up anger. Confronting him with his years of cruelty, she announces her intentions to leave him to go away with Shug, hissing that his "dead body" is precisely "the welcome mat" she needs for her triumphal entry into a new life (181). He tries to stop her, to rob her of her confidence, calling her poor, skinny, ugly, and scared. She draws herself up, refusing his taunts, breaking free of the self-deprecation that has shored up the prison of her despair. "I'm pore, I'm black, and I may be ugly and can't cook," she breathes, with the breath of the Spirit; "But I'm here" (187).

The discovery of meaningful work further emboldens the red thread of Celie's strengthening self-affirmation. Learning to sew "the perfect pair of pants," to market them, to make something and name it after herself even as Shug had earlier made up the snatch of song and named it after her, works wonders of healing old wounds of hopelessness and the aching absence of self-worth. Having, for once in her life, the power to make choices releases her from burial under the desperate weight of necessity. On a crest of assurance, she is able to exult over her remarkable achievements: friends, love, a job, an income, and time to call her own.

But the crest is inconstant, and a new wave of despair washes over Celie at the departure of her friend and beloved, Shug. The red thread of strength temporarily slips out of the pattern of her healing, to be supplanted by an initially faint, but eventually vibrant yellow. The yellow motif is that of discernment, patience, and self-discipline. It is not the yellow of cowardice, but that of the wisdom required to wait for proper times and seasons. Feeling despair over her abandonment, Celie nevertheless does not succumb. She writes to the sister whom she cannot even be sure she will ever see again, affirming that she is either too stubborn or "too crazy" to commit suicide. From the difficulties of her life experiences, Celie has at least learned that the future is unpredictable, and that if unexpectedly bad things can happen, some unexpected good might come along as well.

In the meantime, watching and waiting, Celie undertakes a rigorous project of self-mastery. The pale yellow of discernment turns to vivid gold as she learns not to ask of others the kind of affirmation which she must find from within herself. Gradually, she realizes the futility — worse, the unfairness — of wanting from others what it is not within their power to give. Particularly, she comes to appreciate the importance of letting Shug be herself, even if this means that she chases younger men, even if this means that she is lost to Celie forever. After all, Celie discovers: "Shug got a right to live too. . . . Just cause I love her don't take away none of her rights" (236).

At this disciplined, discerning moment, Celie receives the unexpected news that Shug is coming home. "Now," Celie muses, "Is this life or not?" (247). Having struggled through the possessiveness of her loving, she knows that she can finally be content whether Shug does or does not return. Patience teaches Celie the priceless lesson of how to love within incontestable limits. For Isabel, the victory was learning to love in the face of mortality; for Celie, it is learning to love within the limits of "letting be."

Once again in Celie's life, love — this time, a perfected love — casts out despair. Here her tapestry is emblazoned with the purple threads of community. As the companionship of Nettie and of Shug rescued her early on from the despair of utter loneliness and deprivation, so a culminating reconciliation with Mr. ____ helps win her the ability to look contentedly into the future, even into the prospect of a future without either Nettie or Shug. Thus, it comes as unexpected, undemanded, superabundant gift when both her sister and her woman-friend return to her. In her excess of joy, Celie rushes to embrace an all-inclusive community. "Dear God," she exults: "Dear stars, dear trees, dear sky, dear peoples. Dear Everything. Dear God" (249). Any last vestiges of alienation — from the divine, from other people, from the natural world itself — disappear. Celie has found strength and a discerning love within herself, and has discovered the grace of a communion with all of being. At the end of the densely-woven tapestry of her story, vivid red, yellow, and purple prevail over the chastened and chastening drabness of despair.

Summary

What heals despair? Anyone who has ever suffered from the pains of utter hopelessness knows the anguish of yearning for an answer to the question of healing. It would be so comforting to have a series of therapeutic "How to's" — something on the order of a self-help manual guaranteed to teach techniques for vanquishing despair in six or eight easy lessons. Unfortunately, however, the conquest of despair is no such easy matter. It requires marshaling the multiple dimensions of mind, heart, and will; it requires rousing one's energy at the moment when energy has drained to its lowest ebb. Perhaps most significantly, it requires a subtly dialectical struggle of exertion and grace, recognizing the point at which one's own efforts inevitably fail, being open at that point to receiving the gift of ministrations from another.

Isabel's and Celie's stories, while not providing a manual for the conquest of despair, do provide models for this multi-dimensional, dialectical struggle. *Final Payments* and *The Color Purple* present a phenomenology rather than a physic; they *describe* rather than *prescribe* the means and agencies through which despair meets with healing. Out of these specific descriptions, however, comes a fund of general therapeutic wisdom with potentially widespread applicability.

To summarize this wisdom: to heal despair, it helps to be part of a support community, to have friends and rely upon them, to talk rather than shut oneself off in isolation, to give vent to one's feelings — particularly one's angers. It helps to take pleasure even in seemingly small matters — the succor of the flesh, or the color purple in a field. It helps to have work, modulated by the freedom from having one's identity bound up completely in what one does; it helps to experience the independence occasionally to let oneself and others simply *be*. It helps to take control over those parts of one's life, however minor, which can be changed, all the while recognizing the incontrovertible limits within which no change can realistically be expected. It helps to train oneself in active patience, foregoing the temptation to absolutize present distresses in favor of the humility to await the unanticipated. To heal the pains of despair, from whatever causes, requires the discernment of the mind, the sensitivity of the heart, and the courageous discipline of the will. It also demands, as Isabel's and Celie's stories so beautifully attest, an upsurging or in-breaking of spiritual resources: the epiphany of insight, the empowerment of fellowship, the grace of fresh air breathed into the stifled spaces of the soul.

CHAPTER 2

The Historical Experience:
Patristics, Scholastics,
Reformation, and Renaissance

In the preceding chapter, we looked at the stories of two characters from recent fiction in order to get a preliminary portrait of how despair manifests itself in contemporary experience. Analyzing the stories of Isabel from Mary Gordon's *Final Payments* and Celie from Alice Walker's *The Color Purple* provided some initial answers to a series of key issues: what causes despair, what does it feel like, how does it relate to spirituality, how is it healed? We have not yet, however, directly broached the central issue of whether despair is better categorized as "sin" or "sickness." To approach this question requires looking behind the contemporary experience of despair to its historical manifestations — looking particularly at the portraiture of despair provided in those writings from the Christian tradition which listed it among the progeny of the "seven deadly sins."

In the nineteenth century, Søren Kierkegaard noted with approval that the "old moralists" of the Christian church had shown great wisdom in including despair among the *septem vitia principalis*. Certainly, their wisdom on this score was distinctive: despair had not acquired such derogatory status in other ethical systems of the ancient world. Aristotle's *Nicomachean Ethics* and *Eudemian Ethics*, for example, did not include despair within their lists of vices.[1] In fact, as part of the melancholy temperament described in Aristotelian humoral psychology, despair was considered less a defect than an expected quality of the creative person — the artist, philosopher, or poet.[2] In like manner, the Stoics did not label despair as specifically vicious. While listing hope among the four basic affects, Stoic literature considered the vice associated with a perversion of hope to be not despair, but folly.[3]

Thus, when the Christian moralists stepped onto the scene, their celebration of hope as a *virtue* and their corollary condemnation of despair sounded a genuinely new note in the history of ideas. Reinhold Kuhn points to a similar phenomenon in his historical study of the concept of ennui. He observes that Christianity elevated notions "of minor importance" in earlier psychology "to the status of . . . capital sins."[4] Certainly, despair was so elevated — or lowered, as the case may be. Envisioned as one of the progeny of either *tristitia* or *acedia*, *desperatio* found itself regularly included in the genealogies of vices so popular in early Christian literature. Whether or not it justly deserved such inclusion, and whether or not such inclusion has ethical relevance for contemporary experience — for the lives of people like Isabel and Celie, for example — are issues which remain to be seen. These issues come into clearest focus through an analysis of the treatment of despair in four periods of Christian history: the early or "patristic" age, the medieval or "scholastic" era, the Reformation, and the Renaissance.

The Early Christian Age: Evagrius, Cassian, and Gregory in the Cardinal Sin Tradition

Evagrius Ponticus

Evagrius Ponticus, desert monk of the fourth century, owns a significant position in the history of ideas of despair. He is, in essence, the grandfather of the tradition of the "seven deadly sins." Evagrius' works, the *Antirrheticos* and *Praktikos*, are the first texts to systematize a list of particular "demons" or "destructive passions" to be combatted in the Christian life. His listing of eight such demons initiates the cardinal sin tradition; with some modifications, the list ultimately shrinks from eight to seven, and the terminology shifts from "cardinal" to the slightly more drastic "deadly." The destructive passions of the body which Evagrius identifies are gluttony and impurity; the demonic propensities of the soul include avarice, sadness, anger, *acedia*, vainglory, and pride. Of each of these passions, Evagrius draws a portrait so vivid and perceptive as to catch even the modern reader up short. It is as if he had been listening in at our confessional or, even worse, tuning in to our private thoughts. Of all eight passions, the one which Evagrius most intricately analyzes is *acedia*, the eventual parent sin of despair.

The word *acedia* has no adequate equivalent in English, so it is most often left in the transliterated Greek (alternately spelled *accidia*). Later sin lists in the English-speaking world render the concept as sloth, but this is a serious (and historically significant) reduction in its meaning. *Acedia* includes such features as spiritual "dryness" *(siccitas)*, psychic exhaustion, impatience, alternating restlessness and listlessness, reluctance or outright resentment in the service of one's fellows and of God. Along with other monks of the Egyptian desert, Evagrius frequently identifies the instigator of *acedia* as the "noonday demon," derived from the Psalmist's references to "the destruction that wastes at noonday" (Ps. 91:6).

This demon is particularly dangerous. Listen to some of Evagrius' description:

> The demon of *acedia* — also called the noonday demon — is the one that causes the most serious trouble of all. He presses his attack on the monk [from about mid-morning to mid-day]. First of all he makes it seem that the sun barely moves, if at all, and that the day is fifty hours long. Then he constrains the monk to look constantly out the windows, to walk outside the cell, to gaze carefully at the sun to determine how far it stands from [the hour of dinner], to look now this way and now that to see if perhaps [one of the other monks appears from his cell]. . . .[5]

Anyone who has known the burden of wishing ardently for time to pass, of yearning desperately for something — anything — to happen to interrupt the aridity of the present moment, can resonate with this depiction. Is it, perhaps, the demon of *acedia* who makes clockwatchers of us all? The monk who is prey to this destructive passion finds himself easily offended by his companions, even though he longs for the distractions of their company. He begins to put hatred and blame on the place in which he lives. The noonday demon tempts him to long for some more congenial environment in which to pursue his spiritual vocation, or — what is worse — to abandon that vocation altogether. This canny demon "depicts life stretching out for a long period of time, and brings before the mind's eye the toil of the ascetic struggle, . . . [trying] to induce the monk to forsake his cell and drop out of the fight." Ultimately, the monk under the influence of *acedia* comes to hate "his very life itself." As a victim of the noonday demon, he finds himself driven to despair.

Although the actual word "despair" does not appear in Evagrius' portrait of *acedia*, several of the characteristics which he does name sound sufficiently kindred that we can understand how later genealogies of the "deadly sins" come to designate *desperatio* among its progeny. This holds true for the related sin of sadness (*tristitia*) as well. Here, Evagrius shows keen insight in noting that sadness arises either because of anger (recall Isabel and Celie and the depression which results from their introjected rage) or because of deprivation.[6] Some sadness, he allows, is appropriate, insofar as it issues out of remorse over personal shortcomings on the path to spiritual perfection. However, that sadness which pines away over other deprivations, neglecting to rejoice in the present gifts of God's creation, is insidious. This second form of sadness, like *acedia*, is a demon for the monk to struggle with and overcome.

In the task of overcoming, Evagrius counsels a number of remedial virtues: obedience, continence, fear of the Lord, humility, sorrow for sin, and above all, the insight born of disciplined contemplation — or, to use a word familiar from the study of Isabel and Celie, "discernment." Evagrius urges any monk who is struggling with *acedia* or with sadness to "keep careful watch over his thoughts."[7] Such watch will help him to learn their rhythmic intensities, their accustomed associations, their "periodicity," their order of "rise and fall." The result of this kind of self-scrutiny will be an ability to "name the demons": an ability to recognize the particular circumstances and dynamics in which the "destructive passions" affiliated with the specific demons arise. With this astute recognition, Evagrius advises, we can "address effective words against" the passions that plague us and, in so doing, "pack them off chafing with chagrin and marveling at our perspicacity."[8] Even though the imagery is quaint — a passel of demons, like television commercial roaches alerted to the threat of pesticide, frantic and fuming as they flee from the site of their eviction — there is wisdom here for the modern sufferer, for the person like Isabel or Celie. The wisdom lies in the counsel of patient attention. In pointing to the "periodicity" of the noonday demon and its ilk, Evagrius highlights the fact that afflictions like sadness and *acedia*, even though they feel all-consuming, in actuality are more nearly episodic. They "rise and fall" with particular provocations; although serious, they remain subject to change. Learning to discern the occasions which provoke one to despair, learning to keep those occasions discrete from the overall course of one's life affirmation, is a significant task for disciplined self-mastery. Isabel learns to risk loving, even in the face of mortality; Celie learns to wait for the unexpected to break into the brutal sameness of the present day. Like monks under the onslaught of the noonday demon, individuals in despair fall prey to a serious depletion of their ability to rejoice in the goodness of the creation: this much is sin; but they can also discover contemplative resources to see beyond the immediate moments of their despairing — and therein lies a path to salvation.

John Cassian

If Evagrius Ponticus can be called the grandfather of the tradition of the seven deadly sins, John Cassian can most aptly be termed its father. It is Cassian who translates the wisdom of Evagrian spiritual direction into the context of the western world. Fifth century founder of two monasteries in Marseilles (one for men and one for women), Cassian records his instructions for the monastic life in two key works: *The Foundations of Cenobitic Life and the Eight Capital Sins* and *Conversations with the Fathers*.[9] Both works carry forward the systematic analysis of the vices; both expressly link sadness and *acedia* with despair.

The linkages among sadness, *acedia*, and despair appear most vividly in the genealogical tree of vices which Cassian creates as part of his ethical analysis. Each of the eight cardinal sins on the tree branches into a number of corollary vices. The offshoots of sadness include rancor, bitterness, pusillanimity, and despair. *Acedia* branches off into a collection of ills including indolence, somnolence, stubbornness, curiosity, garrulousness, anxiety, restlessness, and instability of mind and body.[10] Because of the similarities among the parent sins and the progeny of *acedia* and sadness, they are ultimately merged into a single affliction, thereby reducing the list of eight cardinal sins to the more familiar seven.

Interestingly, Cassian — like Evagrius — notes a link between sadness, despair, and anger. This linkage appears in the ordering of the capital sins in his *Foundations of Cenobitic Life*. In this systematic treatise on spiritual development, Cassian ranks the sins according to what he takes to be a certain natural affinity, with each sin seen as growing out of the convolutions or excesses of the one immediately prior to it. His ranking proceeds from the grossest to the most subtle, in the order in which the Christian should tackle them in the struggle toward perfection. The sin of *ira*, or anger, immediately precedes *tristitia* (which immediately precedes *acedia*) in Cassian's ordering. Thus, not only does untreated anger give rise to sadness, which eventuates in the offshoot of despairing. Also, anger must be dealt with before either *tristitia* or *acedia* can have any chanvce of being overcome.

In his analysis of *tristitia*, Cassian (like Evagrius) is careful to distinguish between "good sadness" which comes about as a result of sorrow over one's sins, and "evil sadness" which results when sorrow "changes its object."[11] (Such a distinction at least raises the question of whether there can be such a thing as "good" versus "evil" despair.) To be sad because we feel unworthy of the blessings of heaven is legitimate and laudable; to feel sad because we cannot get what our greed, gluttony, or lust makes us want, however, is illegitimate and indicative of sin.

While the thwarting of a desire may be responsible for "illegitimate" sadness, Cassian is also sensitive enough to recognize that there are times when the origins of our sadness may be harder to trace. *Tristitia*, like despair and *acedia*, can arise "as if spontaneously," "without reason," with "no understandable cause."[12] In noting this, Cassian seems attuned to the kind of free-floating depression which a person sometimes feels without being able to specify why. One of his descriptions is particularly poignant in this regard. In his *Conversation* with Father Daniel, he writes:

> We feel overwhelmed, crushed by dejection [*tristitia*] for which we can find no motif. . . . [Our] train of thought becomes lost, inconstant, and bewildered. . . . We complain, we try to remind our spirit of its original goals. But in vain. Sterility of the soul! And neither the longing for heaven nor the fear of Hell [is] capable of shaking our lethargy.[13]

Certainly, this passage resonates with anyone, ancient or modern, who has felt the pains of "unreasonable" despair, when spiritual peace has inexplicably vanished, leaving no hope for an imminent return.

In such a state of distress, the soul finds itself increasingly disgusted with itself and all its surroundings. Irritable impatience with one's companions grows acute. Unable to concentrate, one begins casting about for diversions. Desires to sleep and to eat arise as overwhelming temptations: mid-morning (the hour of the noonday demon?) brings "such fatigue and such hunger that one feels tired as if one had just traveled a long way or completed a very difficult job, or as if one were exhausted by a complete fast of two or three days!"[14] Torpor and tedium set in. "The confusion of spirit," Cassian writes, "is such that one feels oppressed in darkness." Like Isabel, sleeping and eating furtively in her dismal room; like Celie, lamenting that being alive seems like "an awful strain" — the person in *tristitia/ desperatio/acedia* feels at the very brink of giving up on life.

But surrender, Cassian admonishes, is not the answer: "The assaults of *acedia* must not be evaded by flight, but surmounted by resistance."[15] Patient endurance and courageous struggle are the recommended remedies. We must teach ourselves not to absolutize the present moment; we must gird ourselves to wait and work for better times. Like Isabel and Celie, we must renew our *strength*. As Cassian advises, "*Fortitude* will build up whom *acedia* has laid in ruins."[16] Stern but steadying counsel, this. Manual labor (Celie's pantsmaking) helps; so does concerted meditation on one's future hopes (Isabel's Holy Week reflections), and contemplation of eternal beatitude.[17] Dejection may indeed episodically wash over our spirit. Nevertheless, Cassian's words encourage us to view it as merely temporary and thereby to "tough it through."

Gregory the Great

The last of the Latin "Fathers" of the church, writing a century and a half after Cassian, Gregory stands at a pivotal point in the development of the "seven deadly sins" tradition. More than anyone else, he serves to "de-monasticize" and popularize the concept of the cardinal vices. His most significant works in this regard are *Morals on the Book of Job* and the *Liber Regulae Pastoralis* (the *Pastoral Care*) which establishes guidelines for a ministry of spiritual direction outside the cloister. Gregory is the person responsible for reshaping the sin list into the definitive form which comes to dominate the Latin church, with only occasional exceptions, for the remainder of the concept's theological life. He reduces the number to seven, and merges features of *acedia* and *tristitia* into a single vice, temporarily eliminating the alien Greek word in favor of the latter, more familiar Latin name.[18]

Like Cassian before him, Gregory is fascinated with the systematic scheme of establishing genealogical trees for each of the principal vices. He attributes six "daughters" to his new composite sin of sadness: *malitia* (resistance and hostility), *rancor* (irritability), *pusillanimitas* (cowardice), *torpor circa praecepta* (sluggishness in the pursuit of the good), *vagatio mentis erga illicita* (eagerness to pursue forbidden fruits), and most importantly for present purposes, *desperatio* (despair).[19] Also like Evagrius and Cassian, he notes the relationship between *tristitia* and *ira*: "The sad," he cautions, "are not far from anger."[20]

In his pastoral analysis of the properties and progeny of the various vices, Gregory exerts a profound impact upon a variety of subsequent thinkers. His writings prove particularly important for Søren Kierkegaard. Writing in his journal on July 20, 1839, Kierkegaard observes that "What in certain cases we call 'spleen,' the mystics know under the name of *tristitia* and the Middle Ages under the name *acedia*."[21] To illustrate his point, he cites Gregory's *Morals on Job*, XIII:

> [Sadness] assaults the solitary [person] everywhere. . . . It is lack of interest in things spiritual, slackness of the mind, neglect of religious exercises, hatred of confession, preference for worldly matters.[22]

Kierkegaard commends Gregory's discernment in this passage that the person most likely to be afflicted with sadness or "spleen" is the solitary individual, the person who shuns not only religious confession, but any form of self-unburdening contact with other human beings. Sadness and introversion seem strangely, almost naturally intertwined. Persons alone are more prone to suffer it, yet once under its possession, they are even less likely to confess their distress and need for help (recall Isabel and Celie, and their speechlessness at the deepest pitch of their despairing). Something about sadness (spleen, melancholy) tends to feed and fester on itself and to shun genuine communication. Thus, Kierkegaard pens in the margin beside his quotation from Gregory: "That is what my father called *a silent despair*."[23]

It is at this point that Kierkegaard commends the wisdom of the "old moralists" of the Christian church. He concludes his journal entry on Gregory's analysis of "silent despair" with the remark which has provoked this entire investigation: "It shows a deep knowledge of human nature that the old moralists should have included *tristitia* among the *septem vitia principalis*."[24] Such solitary despondency does have its vicious dimension. Despair — silent or otherwise — depletes the human spirit; it makes all aspirations seem foolish, all actions futile, all human encounters scarcely worth the energy which they consume. Despair kills hope; it makes any prospects of beatitude seem tauntingly out of reach; it slams the door on any potential for grace or newness outside the present circle of pain. Left to fester in silence and solitude, despair can sour into bitterness, resentment, a self-perpetuating self-pity: *rancor, amaritudo, pusillanimitas.* . . . Perhaps the "old moralists" of the cardinal sin tradition did know whereof they spoke.

Focusing on these dispiriting ramifications of *tristitia* and its offspring despair, Gregory introduces a new concept into the list of suggested remedies. Evagrius recommends the discernment born of disciplined contemplation; Cassian counsels fortitude and manual labor. For Gregory, the newly-named virtue which opposes the vice of sadness is "spiritual joy" — *gaudium, laetitia spiritualis*. According to his theories of pastoral care, the best cure for despair is an awareness of the possibilities of grace, a cultivated confidence in God's benevolence and ultimate benediction.

There are times, however, when such confidence is exceedingly hard to come by — times when, despite our best intentions, despair saps our spirits so severely that no amount of pastoral care can convince us of the potentiality for spiritual joy in our own lives. Sounding a new note in the cardinal sins tradition, Gregory at least allows for this experience, attending to the possibility that some forms of despairing may arise more from sickness than from sin. In the *Pastoral Care*, he advises that some people "become gay or sad, not owing to circumstances but to temperament."[25] This single sentence indicates his sensitivity to the issues which animated Greek humoralism. As early as the fifth century B.C.E., Hippocrates had coined the term *melancholia* to indicate an illness caused by an imbalance of black bile, one of the four basic bodily "humors." Several hundred years later, Galen — Greek anatomist and physician of the second century C.E. — expanded upon the Hippocratic theory, designating individual "temperaments" or personality types caused by the preponderance of one of the essential humors. Galen diagnosed *melancholia* as a predisposition to depressive forms of physical infirmity and mental or emotional distress growing out of a native personality "complexion" dominated by the cold, dry, black, bilious humor.[26] In this Hippocratic-Galenic tradition, a person who is born melancholic can scarcely be accused of a "vice" of melancholy; in more modern parlance, a manic-depressive individual cannot fairly or pastorally be held accountable for despondent mood swings. In his caveat about "temperament," Gregory seems at least attuned to such considerations. Nonetheless, he leaves the matter finally unclear. The distinction between vice and psychological disposition, between sin and sickness, awaits more precise delineation in the scholastic era.

The Scholastic Era: Thomas Aquinas

At the high point of scholastic theology, Thomas Aquinas develops the kind of systematic distinction between sinful and amoral despairing which Gregory's work tangentially introduces. Thomas treats of despair in two principal contexts: first, in questions of the *Summa Theologica* dealing with the passions of the human soul (IaIIae: *De passionibus animae*); and subsequently, in his analysis of virtues and vices (in the *Summa* IIaIIae). The former discussion includes despair among the essential dynamics of human emotional life, concluding that, as such, it is neither vice nor virtue. The second discussion gives despair its distinctively Christian moral cast, defining it as a response of aversion to a particular object: the *bonum divinum*, the divine good.

In Thomistic psychology, despair is grouped among the "irascible" passions. The terminology comes from the Latin translation which Thomas used of Aristotle's *De Anima*. According to this source, the appetitive or willing faculty of the human being consists of three parts: the rational or intellectual; and the nonrational or sensory, which is further divided into concupiscible and irascible components. The chart which appears on the next page shows the basic Aristotelian/Thomistic delineation of the passions:[27]

Concupiscible passions, as the chart demonstrates, are those "movements of the soul" which directly target a pleasurable or painful object: desiring it because it is not yet possessed, rejoicing in it when it is acquired; recoiling from it as long as it remains in the future, sorrowing over it when it comes to pass. Because desire is the most keenly felt of any of these "impulse emotions," it lends its name (*concupiscentia*) to the overall faculty.[28]

Frequently, however, obstacles get in the way of our fulfilling our desires. In such instances, we need a higher degree of exertion to acquire a good or avoid an evil; hence, the *irascible*

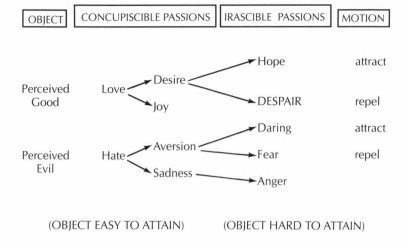

| OBJECT | CONCUPISCIBLE PASSIONS | IRASCIBLE PASSIONS | MOTION |

Perceived Good — Love — Desire — Hope — attract
Love — Joy — DESPAIR — repel

Perceived Evil — Hate — Aversion — Daring — attract
Hate — Sadness — Fear — repel
Sadness — Anger

(OBJECT EASY TO ATTAIN)   (OBJECT HARD TO ATTAIN)

rather than the concupiscible faculty comes into play. *Irascible* passions take their name from anger (*ira*) which is, according to Thomas, the most readily perceived of this type of "contending emotion."[29] Irascibility consists of a powerful and persistent impetus to surmount obstacles in the path of a hard-to-achieve good or a hard-to-avoid evil (*bonum arduum vel malum arduum*).

Within the irascible faculty, there are five primary passions, as shown in the chart. An evil which is difficult to avoid but has not yet happened will result in one of two reactions: daring, if we continue to approach; fear, if we shy away. An evil which is already taking place will give rise to anger, if we can summon the effort to oppose it. (If, on the other hand, we surrender to it, the implicated emotion is sadness, which is no longer a member of the irascible category.In this regard, recall Celie and Isabel, as well as Evagrius, Cassian and Gregory, on the interplay between sadness and anger.) A future good which we think it possible albeit difficult to attain will inspire the contending passion of hope. However, Thomas concludes, "If the object is considered impossible to attain, it becomes repulsive because *when [people] come upon something impossible, they turn away*, according to the *Ethics*." This movement of repulsion "is the reaction of despair, which consists in an act of withdrawal." Despair, like hope, grows out of the dynamics of desire; however, it focuses on impediments to possession rather than on possibilities.

"Hence," says Thomas, "[it] is the contrary of hope as withdrawal is of approach."[30]

Despair as a "withdrawal" of the energy of desiring carries with it a destructive somatic dimension.[31] Thomas reasons: "The emotions which involve an . . . aversion or withdrawal are inimical to the life-motion by the very nature of the way they work, and not just quantitatively." Such emotions depress the spirit, depleting the energies needed to respond to challenges. Like Celie and Isabel, persons under the press of "aversive" emotions find themselves reduced to a mental and physical torpor: not just to the sluggishness in following the commandments (*torpor circa praecepta*) which Gregory diagnoses, but to an all-consuming weariness, a *tedium vitae*, which makes them want to give up on life itself.

It is at this point that the amoral "irascible passion" of despair acquires its first dimension of morality. While neutral in itself, despair as a "contending emotion" can become immoral in accordance with its consequences. In other words, if despair drives a person to some other vice — to gluttony (recall Cassian's monk with the voracious hunger and obsessive eagerness for the arrival of mealtime; recall Isabel's eating frantically, furtively, alone in her room); to hostility toward companions; to violence toward oneself, to the ultimate negation of suicide — then the provoking despair is implicated by association. Further discriminating criteria which Thomas uses in assessing the moral implications of despair include its degree of rationality and volition, and — most significantly for him — its object.

In Thomas Aquinas' scholastic system, there is such a thing as rational despairing. To experience a "movement of withdrawal" from something one realistically recognizes as impossible is a rational act; indeed, continued pursuit of a genuinely "impossible dream" is the perversion of hope which the Stoics knew as "folly." In a sense, then, Isabel is right to give up her hope for utter invulnerability, for a relationship not subject to the limits of mortality; Celie is right to stop hoping that Shug will renounce all her own needs for fulfillment just to keep Celie happy. As W. J. Hill remarks in his commentary on the pertinent passages of the *Summa*, "It would not be a sin . . . to despair about something for which [one] has no capacity at all, or for which [one] is not obligated to strive." To do so, indeed, would be rational — though admittedly, it sounds more as if it would be an act of "resignation" (a withdrawal of energy from a project) than the affect which we customarily intend in modern use of the term "despairing."[32]

The more relevant criterion which Thomas applies in assessing the morality of despair has to do with its degree of volition. Again, Hill's commentary is elucidating.[33] He writes: "A deliberate and positive sin of despair . . . is to be distinguished . . . from indeliberate acts of despair." The category of "indeliberate acts" might account for the behavior of one of Gregory's parishioners with a "melancholic temperament," or the despondent mood swings of a victim of manic-depressive illness. To this category, Hill adds the concept of "semi-deliberate" despairing acts, "such as might arise unbidden and with great suddenness in moments of great melancholy or trial": Isabel's despair upon her father's death, for example, or Celie's despair under her husband's abuse or over her sister's departure. Such traumatic events as these may elicit a momentary, involuntary form of despair; however, when that despair persists past the provoking moment, it is because the individual's will has "consented" to a disposition of despairing. Even so, in the aftershocks of trauma, this consent is only partially deliberate: it is more the product of vulnerability than that of decisive volition. Thus, with regard to such "semi-deliberate" acts of despair, Hill concludes: "Their gravity would not exceed that of venial sin."

The gravity of despair is severely compounded when the criteria of its consequences, its rationality, and its degree of volition are supplemented by the criterion of its object. Despair becomes mortally sinful when its characteristic response of aversion turns away from the particular object of the *bonum divinum*, the "divine good." When it does so, it no longer runs counter to its parallel irascible *passion* of hope, but more seriously, it counters hope as one of the three theological *virtues*. The proper object of the virtue of hope is God and ultimate reunion with the divine. Despair as a *vice* spurns this particular object, rejecting the possibility of living in hopeful affirmation of God's promises of future blessedness. Evelyn Waugh explains why, within the framework of Christian theology, such a rejection is so serious:

> Human beings are made for joy in the love of God, a love which we express in service. If we deliberately turn away from that joy, we are denying the purpose of our existence. The malice of [such an aversion] lies not merely in the neglect of duty (though that can be a symptom of it) but in the *refusal of joy*.[34]

Negating the joy which should accompany hope in God's providence, despair of the divine good is a grievous fault indeed. Still, it constitutes a mortal sin only when a person is fully conscious and deliberate in this rejection.

A major portion of Thomas' treatment of despair as a sin arises in his discussion of the vice of *acedia*. Although he has chosen the Greek name over Gregory's preference for the Latin *tristitia*, Thomas describes the vice in ways which echo his sixth-century predecessor. He, too, ascribes "daughters" to *acedia*, including *desperatio* among them. To the question of whether or not *acedia* is a "chief vice," he responds in the affirmative. Not only does the despair which emanates from *acedia* inhibit moral activity by inducing both physical and mental lassitude. Further, it promotes immoral acts which are committed in order to avoid the spiritual good which one finds distasteful (or simply nonexistent) and to find one's pleasure elsewhere (Gregory's *vagatio mentis erga illicita*). "The loss of hope," Thomas observes "has as its consequence that [people] plunge into evil without restraint and abandon their efforts to do good." He alludes to Proverbs 24:10 ("If you faint in the day of adversity, your strength is small"), warning: "Nothing is more to be avoided than despair, for [the person] who has it loses constancy both in the everyday toils of life and, what is worse, in the struggles of faith." Thus, citing the authority of Isidore of Seville, he concludes: "To perpetrate a crime is a sort of death for the soul, but to despair is to go down into hell."[35]

Because of the extreme gravity of despair, Thomas designates it as one of the six "unforgivable" sins against the Holy Spirit. He cites Augustine as his authority for this designation. A contemporary of Cassian but not a contributor to the cardinal sins tradition, Augustine speaks of despair specifically as a denial of hope in the forgiveness of sin. In Thomas' interpretation, Augustine "says that those who despair of pardon for their sins, or without merits presume on God's mercy, sin against the Holy Ghost."[36] This alliance between despair and presumption is an interesting one; its significance will appear more fully in subsequent chapters, though for now it is important to give Augustine and Aquinas credit for the original insight. Both *desperatio* and *praesumptio* consist of "an assault upon and a destruction of hope."[37] Both the despairing and the presumptuous individual (often one and the same) conclude distrustfully that they know more about what will or will not happen in the future than does God Godself. As a result, the person in despair gives up on any possibilities of grace and new creation, committing an offense against the divine wellspring, hence a "sin against the Holy Spirit." This type of sinful despair is finally "unforgivable": not so much because God cannot or will not forgive it, as because it dully and obdurately refuses to embrace the possibility of forgiveness.

Thomas Aquinas' treatment of despair — as an irascible passion, a daughter of *acedia*, and a sin against the Holy Ghost — is by far the most comprehensive in all the scholastic theology of the medieval era. He clearly defines despair as a form of negative energy — a turning away from a desirable object which is simply deemed too difficult to attain. He sets forth criteria for determining the difference between amoral and immoral acts of despairing: criteria having to do with its consequences, its rationality, its degree of volition, and its object. The one thing which he does not do as explicitly as some of his fellow scholastics is to take into account the occasional physiological causes of despair — to pick up on the tradition of Hippocrates and Galen. John of Wales, for example, identifies "the cold and moist disposition" as a natural cause of *acedia* and its progeny, even as Guillaume d'Auvergne acknowledges that "this vice is sometimes increased and strengthened by the melancholy humor or vapor." David of Augsburg observes that, in such instances, "it behooves the physician rather than the priest to prescribe a remedy."[38] In these three scholastics, more so than in Thomas Aquinas, the understanding of despair as sickness rather than sin begins to gain acceptability within the Christian tradition.

More widespread acceptance, however, awaits the secularizing impulses of the Renaissance, in contrast to the theological radicalization of Reformation thought.

The Reformation: Martin Luther

Martin Luther, instigator of the Reformation, stands at a watershed position in the history of attitudes toward despair within the Christian tradition. On the one hand, he culminates twelve centuries of theological insights into the problem. After him, Protestantism expresses little further interest in the intricate genealogies of cardinal vices through which despair had received attention as an offshoot of *acedia* (or *tristitia*). On the other hand, however, he moves despair to a radically more significant place within his theology: from branch to root, from peripheral importance to the very center of an understanding of Christian experience.

It is possible that despair assumes this key position in Luther's theology because it figures so prominently in his personal struggles. He is subject to episodes of acute depression throughout his life. Some of these episodes are so severe that he confesses, at the mid-point of his career, "I myself have been offended more than once even to the abyss of despair, nay so far as even to wish that I had not been born."[39] In 1527, after a period of physical illness accompanied by devastating throes of doubt and despondency, Luther writes to his friend and follower Melanchthon:

> I was for more than a whole week in death and hell, so that I was sick all over, and my limbs still tremble. I almost lost Christ in the waves and blasts of despair and blasphemy against God.[40]

The intensity of such experiences moves Luther to conclude as to their depth of significance: "One may extinguish the temptations of the flesh; but oh! how difficult it is to struggle against the temptations of blasphemy and despair!"[41]

It is so difficult to struggle against such temptations because despair for Luther is not branch but root, not derivative sin but the very paradigm of Sin itself. According to him, sin has less to do with identifiable and perhaps even superficial acts of vice, and more to do with the profoundest depth of our disrelationship with God. Sin consists of a failure to be sufficiently impassioned in our loyalty to the Being who created us; sin is nothing less than the sobering fact that we do not fulfill the commandment to love the Lord our God with all our heart, soul, mind and strength. Commenting on the radicality of this commandment, Luther confesses, "I don't think there is any faith on earth that could stand face to face with this fact without falling and despairing utterly."[42] Yet, despite such genuine provocation to utter despair, we must not succumb. Or, as Luther puts it in his commentary on the Psalms, "Thou art not even then to despair when thou feelest despair."[43] To do so would merely manifest further an insufficiency of trust in God's promises of mercy. In this way, then, despair constitutes a doubly grave temptation. In comparison with it, the carnal temptations of gluttony, lust, and the other vices on the traditional sin lists appear virtually trivial.

However, in Lutheran thought, despair occupies a profoundly paradoxical position. As he adjures above, we are not to give way to despair even when we feel like despairing. Yet, without an initial movement of despair, we might never be driven to the trust of absolute repentance. Of his own times at the "abyss" when he wished he had never been born, Luther professes: "That is before I knew how beautiful that despair was, and how near to Grace."[44] Where Cassian and others in the cardinal sin tradition also speak of the salutary role of "good" *tristitia* in producing repentance, it is Luther who brings the theme of the positive beauty of despair to its most compelling expression. In spiritual suffering, he writes, the soul "is stripped of its own garment, of its shoes, of all its possessions, and of all its imaginations and is taken away by the Word ... into the wilderness."[45] The pains of despair serve to strip the soul of any pretentions to sanctity, casting it into utter, naked dependence upon God's gracious mercy. While spiritually agonizing, such pains constitute the most profound human mirroring of "the sufferings of the cross."[46]

The crucifixion, indeed, is the focal point for Luther's understanding of Christ, in light of which it appears quite fitting that despair is a key moment in his theological understanding of human reality. Jesus on the cross embodies the ultimate paradigm of a human being in the anguish of despair — a despair issuing from the most extreme and excruciating sense of divine abandonment. Consequently, to attend in faith to "Christ and Him crucified" is to be made radically aware of how God Godself is present with us in our sufferings, even at the deepest pitch of desperation — "bearing our griefs and carrying our sorrows" (Isaiah 53), lifting us up into the very heart of the divine co-suffering (the etymological meaning of "com-passion"). In the throes of our anguish, we are — like Christ — to "cry unto God," giving voice to our uncomprehending abandonment. My God, my God, what is the meaning of this? Why me? How long, oh Lord, how long? Such cries will be heard, Luther is confident. He assures: "There are none nearer to God in this life than this kind of haters and blasphemers of him, nor any [children] more pleasing to [God] and beloved by him."[47]

Such reassurances offer one type of healing for despair. Luther also offers some sterner counsel. "Depression and melancholy proceed from the devil," he concludes; "of this I am quite certain."[48] Consequently, the further remedies for despair which he proposes attempt to take the particular potency of the devil's wiles into account. "The darts of the devil cannot be removed pleasantly and without effort when they are so deeply embedded in your flesh," Luther warns a despairing friend:

> They must be torn out by force. Accordingly, you must be resolute, bid yourself defiance, and say to yourself wrathfully, "Not so, good fellow. No matter how unwilling you are to live, you are going to live and like it! This is what God wants, and this is what I want too. Begone, you thoughts of the devil! To hell with dying and death! . . ." Grit your teeth in the face of your thoughts, and for God's sake be more obstinate, headstrong, and willful than the most stubborn peasant or shrew.[49]

The tooth-gritting defiance which Luther recommends here (akin to Cassian's call for fortitude and resonant with Isabel's and Celie's struggles for self-mastery and strength) is not intended to suggest that one can overcome demonic depression by brute effort of the will alone. "If you impose such demands on yourself and fight against yourself in this way," he continues,

"God will assuredly help you."[50] However, if there are no vigorous efforts and opposition, the torments of Satan will take over in short order, and all remaining possibilities of faith and hope will be tragically lost.

On other occasions, Luther counsels less a hard-line stance of defiant opposition to the devil, and more a position of brash and almost blithe disregard. In some instances of temptation, one should "laugh [one's] adversary to scorn" and conquer the devil "by mocking and despising him, not by resisting and arguing with him."[51] In addition to such mockery, music also proves to be an effective medicine against Satan: "for the devil is a saturnine spirit, and music is hateful to him, and drives him far away from it."[52] Humor, playfulness, conviviality, and even certain kinds of indulgence can further be effectively employed. "When the devil pesters you with [depressing] thoughts," Luther writes another friend, "at once seek out the company of [others], drink more, joke and jest, or engage in some other merriment."[53] Get on horseback and go out hunting; get engrossed in work of some kind; get downright angry; if need be, think of an attractive woman (or an attractive man?).[54] That such counsels are effective is amply illustrated by the vital roles played by work, anger, companionship, and the legitimation of various pleasures in both Isabel's and Celie's healing epiphanies. As Roland Bainton remarks regarding these audacious measures among Luther's suggested remedies for despair, they are "in a way prescribing faith as a cure for the lack of faith." In other words, to refuse to argue with Satan, to abandon confrontation in favor of the diversions of companionship, work, sport, music, merriment, or drink "is of itself an act of faith akin to the *Gelassenheit* of the mystics, an expression of confidence in the restorative power of God, who operates in the subconscious" while we occupy ourselves with "extraneous things."[55] In short, to seek pleasure over despair is to rely on the steady goodness of God's creation which sustains us through transient temptations to nihilism.

Luther tries to follow his own advice on this score. "I myself," he confesses, "who have passed all my former life in melancholy and depression of spirit, now accept joy and happiness wherever they present themselves — nay, go in search of them."[56] To do so is pleasing to God, who created the world for our joy and thanksgiving. In avoidance, disregard, or outright defiance of despair, Luther enjoins us to "be merry . . . both inwardly in Christ and outwardly in his gifts and the good things of life. . . . It is for this that he provides his gifts — that we may use them and be glad, and that we may praise, love, and thank him forever and ever."[57] What God wants of us is not simply our obedience, but our joy: a full-bodied, whole-hearted, whole-souled rejoicing sufficient to cast out depression and despair.

In all honesty, however, Luther acknowledges that such joy is not as simple as it sounds. We are, in fact, commanded to "rejoice always" (I Thess. 5:16); "I now preach this, and I also write it," Luther confesses, "but I haven't as yet learned it."[58] Life in this fallen world seems to breed countless occasions for despairing. When the diversions and gratifications of the flesh will not suffice to facilitate therapeutic and thankful joyousness, we must seek stronger spiritual medicine. In the final analysis, for Luther, such ills as fear, anxiety, depression, melancholy, doubt, and despair require the cure of trust in the graciousness of God. Scripture reading, prayer, and attention to God's word as communicated by a clergyperson or a caring neighbor all serve to bolster such trust. "The best remedy of all," Luther says, "without which all the rest are as nought," is "to believe firmly in Jesus Christ."[59]

Because of the complex linkages between despair and faith, Luther ultimately concurs with Thomas Aquinas and with Augustine in designating despair an unforgivable sin against the Holy Ghost. No offering of God's mercy will suffice to forgive us if we resolutely refuse to trust in the very possibility of our forgiveness. Such a refusal reveals the integral relation between despair and presumption, vices which Aquinas placed together and which continue to be paired in Luther's judgment. To renounce the possibility of grace is to foreclose on the divine mercy with a presumptuous assumption that our own assessment of a situation is superior to God's. Or, as Luther puts it: "Sin carries us down to despair or up to presumption. In either case the sin is not repented of, for sin is either exaggerated or not acknowledged at all."[60] Clearly, he is speaking here of despair directed towards a particular object — that is, of despair of the forgiveness of sins. However, his insight seems to have applicability as well to a more broadly targeted despair over personal unworthiness. For Isabel to despair because she feels her existence apart from her invalid father to be purposeless; for Celie to despair because she feels that apart from Shug and Nettie she is nothing; for any of us to despair because we feel in our gut that we are just not "good enough" (for "good," read any of a number of descriptive terms: not sufficiently smart, thin, attractive, talented, prosperous, productive, upwardly-mobile . . .) constitutes, in a profoundly paradoxical way, an exaggeration of personal importance: a presumptuous projection of personal assessments onto the world at large; a desire to do all and be all, all by one's self; a conclusion that if one cannot succeed in this inflated task of self-justification, one's existence must not be justified at all. Keenly appraising this paradox, Luther stresses over and over the difficult but despair-defeating wisdom that ultimate acceptability depends not on one's own merit, but rather on grace.

Thus, Luther differs from the majority of his predecessors in the sin tradition on the essential point that his stress on grace calls the very underpinnings of that tradition into question. The notion of particular headings and branches of vice to which particular remedial virtues can be applied becomes for him deceptive, at best, and at worst completely destructive. Rather than specific sins — like *acedia, tristitia, ira,* and the rest — the real problem of human existence has to do with Sin itself: the tragic disruption of relationship between creatures and their Creator, which gives rise to an ever-defective trust, hope, joy, and devotion. Despair speaks as a pointedly painful witness to the fact that we constantly fail to love God with all our heart, soul, mind, and strength. The only remedial virtue which can finally compensate for this failure is that of *faith* — and this virtue itself is not an accomplishment of ascetic discipline, but rather a free gift, through the grace of God in Christ.

Despair, therefore, figures at the very heart of Luther's theology of Christian existence. To experience it is to experience the need for grace at its greatest intensity; to dwell in it is to deny grace and to cast oneself into the torments of hell. For Luther, grace can appear through the succor of the flesh — the fragrance of spices, the color purple in a field; laughter, music, the voice of a ministering friend. Or it can appear through the solace of the spirit — the in-breaking epiphany of divine compassion, embracing the soul's aching loneliness in the outreach of everlasting arms. Either way, there is healing to be had. His assurances ring with truth, because his confessions of his own spiritual crises ring with such poignant authenticity. Of them, he writes:

> In this state, hope despairs and despair hopes: and there is nothing remaining alive but that inward groan that cannot be uttered in which the Spirit rises, moving upon the face of these waters covered with darkness. . . . No one can understand these things but he [or she] who has tasted them: they do not stand in speculations. . . . They lie in the inmost feelings of the soul.[61]

Yet, having tasted these torments, he is able to add: "Just when I was in death's deepest throes and had the least hope,... the Lord came . . . and by a miracle led my life out of death and destruction."[62] Luther's deeply personal theology is utterly convinced that the Spirit moves over the turbulent chaos of the human heart, answering the sin of despair with the gift of new creation.

Renaissance Humanism: Robert Burton

In the sixteenth century, a very different mindset regarding despair coexists alongside Luther's theological radicalism. For Luther, despair epitomizes the root of Sin itself: estrangement from God and the resultant inability to live in joyful trust amidst the gifts of the creation. While recommending a variety of earthy and earthly remedies, he ultimately assumes that final healing for despair requires divine grace; when despair is sin, healing must entail redemption. In contrast to this position stands the perspective of Renaissance humanism — a perspective which increasingly moves issues of sin and salvation out of the forefront in its analysis of human experience. A secular focus supersedes the theocentric emphases of Luther, Thomas Aquinas, and the cardinal sins tradition; natural explanations supplant the supernatural. The Renaissance humanist understanding of despair provides a telling case in point.

We have heard hints of naturalistic explanations in a few previous places — Gregory the Great in his remarks about temperament, some scholastic theologians other than Thomas in their willingness to give some moments of despair a physiological etiology. These hints swell to a leitmotif in the sixteenth and seventeenth centuries. A whole genre of Renaissance literature renews interest in the Greek tradition of Hippocrates and Galen, elaborating and popularizing "medical" analyses of the physiological causes and cures for the disease of melancholy, which now has primacy of place in discussions of despair over the older "parental" vices of *acedia* and *tristitia*.[63]

The most ambitious and comprehensive example of this literary genre is a 1621 treatise by Robert Burton, something of the scope of which can be discerned in its title: *The Anatomy of Melancholy: What it is, with all the kinds, causes, symptomes, prognostickes, and severall cures of it. . . . Philosophically, Medicinally, Historically opened and cut up.*[64] Burton tips his hand as to the predominantly naturalist, secular intent of his work in the preface to his book: "My purpose and endeavour," he writes, "is . . . to anatomize this humour of melancholy, through all its parts and species, as it is an habit, or an ordinary disease."[65]

He cannot quite stick to this program, however. In addition to being a self-styled "anatomist," Burton is also an Anglican clergyman, or "Divine." Thus, his medical treatise comprises an underlying moral intent; he aims to provide his readers with the knowledge necessary for virtuous as well as healthy living. The two go hand in hand, he is convinced. Particularly in the case of despair, the resources of medicine and of moral suasions are needed. "A Divine in this compound mixed malady," he confesses, "can do little alone, a Physician in some kinds of melancholy much less." The two — Divine and Physician — must work together and "use diverse medicines to cure":

> one amends the soul through the body, the other the body through the soul. . . . One helps the vices and passions of the soul, anger, lust, desperation, pride, presumption, etc., by applying spiritual physick; as the other uses proper remedies in bodily diseases.

Insofar as melancholy is "a common infirmity of body and soul" which "hath as much need of a spiritual as a corporal cure," Burton recommends himself for its treatment, as one who is "by my profession a Divine, and by mine inclination a Physician."[66] His analysis of "kindes, causes, symptomes, prognostickes, and cures" therefore proceeds on two fronts, which are not always clearly differentiated or integrated in his own thinking. He straddles the fence between theological and physiological explanations, but for our purposes it is the newly dominant motif of physiology which is the more engaging.

For Burton, despair is related to melancholy as a specific and particularly pernicious variant of the broader classification. In Part II of the *Anatomy*, speaking of "definite" or humoral forms of melancholy, he notes that these are related to the "irascible appetite" (recall Thomas) and can degenerate, at their most serious, into madness and despair.[67] In Part III, dealing with "indefinite" melancholy, Burton diagnoses despair as "opposite to hope, that sweet Moderator of Passions," which makes it a most dangerous and life-threatening disease. "Of . . . melancholy Symptoms," he concludes, "these of Despair are the most violent, tragical, and grievous."[68] The despairing "are in great . . . distraction of soul, restless, full of continual fears, cares, torments, anxieties"; fear "dries [their] blood, wasteth the marrow, alters their countenance"; their critical affliction "consumes [them] to nought."[69]

Causes of this specific affliction can be natural or supernatural, for Burton; the former and newly distinctive category merits our closest attention. Natural causes include such "inward, congenital" influences as age, heredity, and temperament, and such "outward, adventitious" disturbances as "terrors, frights, calumnies, servitude, imprisonment, poverty, want, accident, death and loss" — not to mention disease or distemper of particular bodily parts.[70] (Note how many of the preceding conditions are applicable to Isabel's and Celie's experiences.) Humoral factors take on particular significance: the cold, dark humor of black bile (the literal root of *melan-cholia*) produces fumes that corrupt healthy mental and spiritual functioning. "When the humour is stirred up," Burton notes, "every small object aggravateth and incenseth it." Sensitivity to tragedy and vulnerability to despair are acutely heightened by fatigue, illness, the accumulation of stresses, the depletion of energy, and other "stirrings ups" of the sources of melancholy.[71] Akin to Gregory, Burton notes the pastoral importance of attending to such possible natural causations:

> To give some satisfaction to melancholy [people] that are troubled with these symptoms, a better means in my judgment cannot be taken than to shew them the causes whence they proceed; not from Devils, as they suppose [Evagrius' theories of the noonday demon notwithstanding!], or that they are bewitched or forsaken of God . . . as many of them think but from natural and inward causes.[72]

Knowing these causes, the sufferer may then invoke the aid of a physician and find some remedy for his or her distress.

The physician has various remedial measures to apply. First, the pharmaceutical. "There be those that prescribe Physick [in cases of 'distemper of humours']," Burton writes: "'Tis God's instrument, and not unfit. The Devil works by mediation of humours, and mixt diseases must have mixt remedies." Thus, it is not inappropriate "to set down certain Amulets, herbs, and precious stones, which have marvelous virtues all." In the same manner, "suffumigations" with "many simples," with sulphur, wine, bitumen, castor oil, and so forth may be effectively employed. Bloodletting and purgation can prove useful in dispelling bad humors; proper diet and evacuation are essential; "alteratives" and "comfortatives" may serve respectively to "thin" black bile, and to cheer the spirits and "enliven" the blood.[73]

In conjunction with these physiological remedies, certain psychological and philosophical measures further exert an "enlivening" and restorative influence on the patient in despair. Like Luther, Burton commends "strong drink, mirth, musicke, and merry company" to stir up the blood and "attenuate" depressive humors.[74] Sports and social gatherings have similarly beneficial effects. "Let [the despairing person] ease the soul by honest recreations," Burton counsels, in order to "refresh and recreate his [or her] distressed soul."[75] A disciplined life of self-examination can conduce to greater self-control and less subjection to temporal sorrows. Confession to a friend can further lighten the despair-producing burden on one's spirit. Above all, Burton says, echoing in interesting ways the warnings of Cassian from within the monastic tradition:

> Only take this for a . . . conclusion, as thou tendest . . . thy good health of body and mind, observe this short Precept, give not way to solitariness and idleness. Be not solitary, be not idle.[76]

Otiositas, idleness, one of the original progeny of *acedia* — the offspring, indeed, most honored by the eventual English rendering of this cardinal sin as "sloth" — here receives decisive attention as a component of Elizabethan melancholy and despair. Fortunately for the sufferer, this dimension of the malady can be cured by the plain old virtue of busyness. *Ora et labora*: pray and work. Celie's pantsmaking participates in a longstanding therapeutic tradition!

Thus, while Burton stands most firmly in the Greek tradition of Hippocrates and Galen in his emphasis on despair as a humoral disorder accessible to physical cure, he also participates in the Christian moral tradition which sees irreducible dimensions of cure to reside in virtue-animated living. Burton's humanism remains, after all, the Christian humanism of the Renaissance, and not the totally secularized version which does not emerge until later centuries. With an appreciation for the complex spiritual as well as physical dimensions of despairing, he notes how "They take a wrong course that think to overcome this feral passion by sole Physick."[77] Avoiding idleness, enlivening the spirits, observing a daily regimen which is conducive to "good health of body and mind" — all these preventive or remedial measures are important, but none are finally sufficient for the most radical forms of despair. There are times when the diversions of music, merry-making, companionship, and busyness prove to no avail, when despair so consumes its sufferers that "even in their greatest delights, singing, dancing, dalliance, they are still . . . tortured in their souls."[78] At these times, when none of our efforts seem able to break through the tedium which has settled in our spirit, we are left to rely on an epiphany — a gift, a grace, breaking in upon us from beyond those limited resources which we can claim as our own.

For such extreme instances, Burton prescribes a seven point program to pursue toward healing:

1. Acknowledge that all help comes from God;
2. Acknowledge that the source of one's misery is sin;
3. Repent and be heartily sorrowful;
4. Pray for the easing of one's distress;
5. Implore the prayers of the Church;
6. Apply the remedies of Physick;
7. Rely on God's mercy.[79]

Characteristically, even here in Burton's intentionally theological discourse, the physiological dimension — application of the remedies of Physick — is not omitted. What is even more interesting is the fact that Burton is not naive about the ease of any of these measures — physical or spiritual — for procuring health. Most people in despair, he admits, are "too sorely afflicted" to be able to do the majority of these things.[80] Indeed, such is precisely the problem with the perversity of this particular malaise. If we simply *could* acknowledge God as the source of help and prayerfully rely on divine mercy, we would likely not be in despair in the first place! As Roland Bainton insightfully noted of Luther, so Burton in the final analysis here is recommending "faith as a cure for the lack of faith." Disturbing as this recommendation may be for those of us who would really rather be able to heal ourselves, it does carry a certain ring of existential truth: more often than not, when we feel ourselves emerging from despair, we can point less to any remedial program that we have accomplished than to the simple (miraculous, mercy-full) fact that we somehow find ourselves refreshed and renewed.

Despair for Burton, then, is finally both sin and sickness, although he attends more concertedly to its medical component than anyone before him in the Christian tradition. If there is one overarchingly valuable function fulfilled by the "compound mixt" treatise of *The Anatomy of Melancholy* in its discussion of the "compound mixt malady" of despair, it is this: despite its occasional confusion about the relation between natural and supernatural causes and cures for despairing, Burton's work slowly and circuitously searches out the contours of the problem. By identifying all those elements of despair which are provoked by natural "congenital" and "adventitious" causes and which can therefore be remedied by "physick" or other human cure, he serves to locate the deep root of the affliction which is finally inaccessible to solely human remediation. In beginning and in ending his treatise, he articulates an awareness of the fundamental brokenness of the human condition which is described in theological language by the concept of "original sin." For Burton the "anatomist" and Anglican Divine, this brokenness finally implores assistance from beyond human capabilities, from the ministrations of a Divine Physician, "as our Saviour calls himself, and was indeed."[81]

Conclusion

Despair: sin or sickness? A variety of responses to this dilemma emerge out of the history of the Christian tradition. For Evagrius, despair is preeminently the product of the noonday demon who distracts and disheartens us and whom we send "chafing away" with our practice of disciplined contemplation. For Cassian, despair is an offshoot of *acedia* and sorrow, both cardinal vices; it gives voice to the anguished outcry, "Sterility of the soul!" and demands the bracing countermeasures of fortitude and manual labor. For Gregory, despair opposes spiritual joy; it festers in solitude and shuns potentially restorative community; it requires attentive pastoral care, except perhaps when it is more a temperamental than a spiritual affliction. For all of these "old moralists" of the Christian church, despair is first and foremost a sin: it distracts us from virtue, and it demonstrates our failure to live steadfastly and joyously devoted to the service of God.

In contrast to this unilateral assessment, Thomas Aquinas offers a more systematic and nuanced understanding. In his *Summa*, despair ranges from being an amoral passion of the irascible appetite, to being an offshoot of the vice of *acedia*, to being one of six unforgivable sins against the Holy Spirit. He establishes criteria to differentiate among these categories:

criteria of consequences, rationality, volition, and object. The last-mentioned criterion is particularly significant for distinguishing relatively innocuous despair over something earthly from the *summum malum* of despair over the divine good.

Luther and Burton, Reformation and Renaissance thinkers respectively, approach the dilemma of despair less systematically than Thomas Aquinas, their medieval scholastic forerunner. Nonetheless, both share insights with Thomas and other predecessors in the Christian tradition as well as introducing distinctive flavorings of their own. For Luther, despair is not *a* sin, but Sin itself, a breach of trust; earthly diversions can be effective against it, but ultimately the source of healing is God's grace. For Burton, while the motif of sin and grace remains present, a largely new emphasis emerges: despair is a sickness of the melancholy humor, resultant from natural causation and amenable to "Physick cure."

The century of Burton's death is also the century in which modern science takes off in earnest: William Harvey discovers the circulation of the blood; Anton van Leeuwenhoek pioneers work with the microscope; Isaac Newton posits the theory of universal gravitation. Increasingly, the world seems to run as a self-regulating machine, with the human body as one complex mechanism within it. Renaissance humanism with its continued willingness to acknowledge divine intervention gives way to an "enlightened" and secularized humanism which has no room for God whatsoever. The eighteenth century French astronomer and free-thinker Laplace boldly summarizes the emerging world view: "God? I have no need of that hypothesis."[82]

The resultant reduction of human complaints to medical and scientific problems represents both gain and loss. To be sure, it is better that the remedies of "Physick cure" be appropriately applied than that prayers for forgiveness be indiscriminately prescribed as a panacea. It is far better to be diagnosed as "sick" with depression than to be accused of demon possession and burned at the stake! The turn from theological to medical and psychological therapies for mental or emotional disturbances has signaled a tremendous advance in human tolerance and self-understanding.

And yet. . . . If there are advantages to the secularized "triumph of the therapeutic," there were advantages to the theologized reliance upon divine redemption as well.[83] To the person with genuinely felt religious questions — of guilt and forgiveness, emptiness and meaning, fate and providence — the reassurances of secular humanism speak not at all, except to belittle the questions as deluded and misplaced: a dubious comfort at best. Even to persons whose questions do not fall into traditional religious categories and vocabulary, the solutions proposed by rationalistic philosophy or by medical and psychological science may at times come up sorely lacking. What do we do, for example, with the despair that results when the various therapies have all been attempted, but to no avail? What do we do with the pervasive dis-ease of mind and heart for which we can search out no discernible cause and which yields to no practicable cure? What do we do with the ache of aloneness and anguishing responsibility which follows upon being told that the human is all we have, and that we must therefore actualize our capabilities for self-healing, simply rising above any pains and perturbations which we cannot otherwise master? What do we do when our will is wearied, and what we really yearn for is grace?

Such human and, at heart, religious queries never disappear completely from the history of ideas, although they may go underground for a time. In the nineteenth century, after many years of neglect, they re-emerge with searing clarity in the works of Søren Kierkegaard. Looking respectfully to the "old moralists" of the Christian church, Kierkegaard struggles to reawaken an appreciation for the profoundly theological depths of causation and cure belonging to despair — which he terms both "sin" and "the sickness unto death." It is to his insights which we now turn in Chapter Three.

CHAPTER 3

The Sickness unto Death:
Kierkegaard's Analysis

As we have just seen, for the "old moralists" of the Christian church, despair is a sin, while for Burton it is on its way to becoming an illness which can be remedied by natural cures. But for a distinctly separate strand in the history of ideas, despair is neither sin nor sickness; rather, it is evidence of a laudable sensitivity of spirit. The *Oxford English Dictionary* notes that "in the Elizabethan period and subsequently, the affectation of melancholy [is] a favourite pose among those who [make] a claim to superior refinement."[1] The Romantic era carries forward this strand of exaltation. Spiritual suffering acquires a kind of voluptuousness in the figure of the swooning Romantic hero. The French coin a name for such suffering: *mal du siècle* ("century-sickness"); the English refer to it, more in the medical tradition of Hippocrates and Galen, as "spleen."

Judge William, pseudonymous author of Volume Two of Søren Kierkegaard's *Either/Or*, comments pointedly on this romanticizing tendency: "No intoxication is so beautiful as despair, so becoming, so attractive, especially in maidens' eyes," he writes. "In our time . . . to be melancholy is the dignity to which everybody aspires."[2] Kierkegaard himself deplores such aspirations, even as he spurns the trend to "medicalize" despair in neglect of its theological ramifications. His contrasting analysis of despair as radically sinful thus appears to be markedly out of step with its times. Kierkegaard would be pleased with such an assessment. After all, he would ask, what could possibly be the benefit of being "in step" with a generation which is rushing headlong to disaster?

However out of step *The Sickness Unto Death* may be with the mood of nineteenth century Romanticism, it is thoroughly in keeping with those "old moralists" of the Christian church whose knowledge of human nature Kierkegaard applauds. What is more, it is remarkably congruent with "the contemporary experience" of despair such as we find in the stories of Isabel and Celie. To careful and courageous readers (for it is often a daunting text), *The Sickness Unto Death* holds up a startling mirror. We see ourselves in Kierkegaard's depictions of despairing. Amazed by the resemblance, we cannot help but wonder how he, living in so different an era, could have known us so well.

Kierkegaard writes frequently about despair. His life's story has justly earned him the epithet of "melancholy Dane." Like Robert Burton who confesses in the opening pages of the *Anatomy* that he "writ of melancholy, by being busy to avoid melancholy," so perhaps Søren Kierkegaard writes of despair in an attempt to exorcise his own propensity to despairing.[3] (For that matter, can we deny a kindred motivation in ourselves — in my writing, or your reading, of this book?) *Either/Or*, the *Journals, Purity of Heart Is to Will One Thing, Training in Christianity* — all include discussions pertinent to despair and its conquest. By far the most comprehensive treatment, however, appears in the book to which I have already been alluding: *The Sickness Unto Death*. In this work, Kierkegaard divides his analysis into two major parts. "Part First, That Despair Is the Sickness Unto Death" comprises a phenomenological description of the diverse forms of despairing experienced by the "humanist" self. "Part Second, Despair Is Sin" presents a theological critique of despair as it exists in the "self before God." These divisions will form the basic outline for the present chapter, immediately following a word of clarification about the definition of despair in Kierkegaard's distinctive lexicon.

For the majority of the authors just examined in the history of ideas of despair within the Christian tradition, the etymology of despair is a Latinate one: *de-speratio* stands counter to *spes* or hope (as fourteenth-century English used the now-archaic word *wanhope* to designate hope's opposite). Kierkegaard is certainly aware of the Romance root and what it implies (in his journals, for example, he cites Gregory the Great in the original Latin). Writing in Danish, however, he is also privy to another set of etymological implications. Like the German *Verzweiflung*, the Danish *Fortvivlelse* is built around a key term meaning not "hope," but "two" (*Zwei, Tvi*).[4] Akin to "doubt" (*Tvivl*), despair emerges out of a fundamental "doubleness" or "dividedness" in the human spirit. Despair gives evidence to the fact that the human self consists of a difficult synthesis of warring dualities: Kierkegaard labels them finitude/infinity and necessity/possibility. The components of these dualities coexist in perpetual tension and imbalance, for which reason we find ourselves continually to be "out of joint." Thus, in Kierkegaard's lexicon, despair implies not only the absence or rejection of hope, but also the brokenness symptomatic of a chronic dis-equilibrium and dis-ease: a sickness so disabling that it is aptly described as "unto death."

Phenomenology of Despair

In Kierkegaard's analysis, there are gradations of despair. Certainly, this rings true to experience. I know that there are days when I wake up sensing a kind of nagging discoloration of my worldview; everything looks slightly "off" to me, slightly jaundiced, though if anyone were to ask what was wrong, I would be hard-pressed to name a particular provocation for my general discontent. I might even be surprised by the question, not having given conscious attention to the fact that I was feeling and acting out of sorts. This is an initial gradation of despairing. On the other hand, there are moments when a very precise, very profound pain shoots through me, when a mass of identifiable pressures and provocations finally comes to a head and I cry out, "This is it; this is all I can take; I really don't think I can stand any more." This is a more acute gradation of despair. The former level is akin to Celie's general numbness under the

oppressions of her father and her husband, before she has even allowed herself to look too closely at the inequities of her situation. The latter level comes after she has been awakened to her own anger, after Nettie is gone and Shug has left and "Being alive begin to seem like an awful strain."
The Sickness Unto Death names both these unconscious and acutely conscious gradations of despair. In fact, Kierkegaard adds a variety of nuances at each level. He refers to the gradations which he identifies as "levels of potentiation": in other words, as we move from level to level, our despair becomes progressively more all-encompassing, more serious, and more self-aware. The following schematic shows the levels of potentiated despair as Kierkegaard discusses them in *The Sickness Unto Death*:

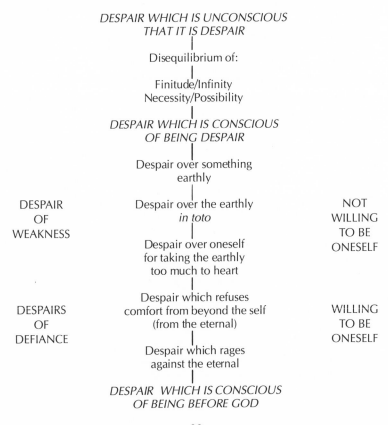

DESPAIR WHICH IS UNCONSCIOUS THAT IT IS DESPAIR

Disequilibrium of:

Finitude/Infinity
Necessity/Possibility

DESPAIR WHICH IS CONSCIOUS OF BEING DESPAIR

Despair over something earthly

DESPAIR OF WEAKNESS	Despair over the earthly *in toto*	NOT WILLING TO BE ONESELF
	Despair over oneself for taking the earthly too much to heart	
DESPAIRS OF DEFIANCE	Despair which refuses comfort from beyond the self (from the eternal)	WILLING TO BE ONESELF
	Despair which rages against the eternal	

DESPAIR WHICH IS CONSCIOUS OF BEING BEFORE GOD

We will follow Kierkegaard's order of presentation as we look into the mirror which he holds up to our experience.

Unconscious Despair

We noted that a root meaning of despair in Danish is "two," and that Kierkegaard's analysis of the experience consequently draws upon his conviction of the dividedness or disequilibrium of human selfhood. In his estimation, this disequilibrium occurs in two pairs of polarities: the polarity of infinity and finitude, and that of possibility and necessity. When either side of one of these polarities is given undue emphasis, a form of despair — albeit a largely unconscious one — is the result.

(If a few of these descriptions sound like some condition other than despair to us, we must recall that Kierkegaard's language and lexicon imbue his interpretation with some distinctive shades of meaning.)

The despair of infinity results when a person's feelings, knowledge, and will lose touch with the finite limits of concrete reality and become "fantastic" (flighty, vacuous, groundless — whatever the opposite of "down to earth" would be). "When feeling becomes fantastic," Kierkegaard writes, "the self is simply volatilized more and more, at last becoming a sort of abstract sentimentality which . . . does not apply to any person, but . . . participates feelingly . . . in the fate of one or another abstraction, e.g. that of mankind *in abstracto*."[5] (I said earlier that the text could be daunting!) What Kierkegaard is describing here is the same situation depicted in the famous Peanuts cartoon where Charles Schulz has Linus exclaim: "I love mankind; it's people I can't stand." We can all find it fairly easy to feel sympathy for the poor starving masses in some far-away country; it is more difficult for us to address the threatening economic inequities right in our own backyard. The despair of infinity thus beckons us. (Interestingly enough, it is a form of the despair of infinity that Isabel initially seeks in her attempt to love abstractly and disinterestedly, eschewing the vulnerability of particular affections.)

Not only feeling, but also knowledge and will can become thus detached from their finite moorings. We can speculate brilliantly about the psychological mechanisms at work in other people's foibles, all the while remaining shockingly blind to the reality of our own. We can cook up grandiose schemes which have no hope of becoming reality because we do not anchor them in any concrete steps toward actualization. While each of us can probably catch ourselves in moments of the despair of infinity once we know what we are looking for, most of the time we remain largely unconscious of our "fantastic" and "volatilized" distortions. Indeed, according to Kierkegaard, a whole generation lived naively in a state of such disequilibration during the excesses of the Romantic era.

The despair of disequilibrated possibility is very similar to the despair of infinity. In both cases, the sufferer (who is only minimally aware of being a sufferer) loses a hold on the limits imposed by the concrete — the given, the finite, the necessary. Although it may not initially seem so, too much possibility can generate as many problems as too little. The phenomenon of "overchoice" which Alvin Toffler described years ago in his analysis of *Future Shock* gives contemporary terminology to this condition.[6] My own favorite, if trivial, example comes from the act of buying a toothbrush (Toffler's description is of buying a car, which may say something of the differential levels of our purchasing power): do I want three or four rows of bristles; hard, medium, or soft; natural or — what? unnatural?; angled head or straight; a color I like, or a color to match my bathroom walls? Even at this silly level, I can experience a kind of paralysis bordering on panic as I face the need to make a choice among a surfeit of possibilities.

How much more so, then, in the weightier decisions of personal or professional life? I regularly see students who are members of what I call the "Major of the Month Club" — they flit from subject matter to subject matter as their enthusiasms carry them, but they cannot muster the gritty determination to root in any one area for too very long. (Surely this whole phenomenon has been exacerbated by the multi-channel options, changeable with a flick of the dial, of cable TV!) Nor does this affliction limit itself to members of the academic community. The feeling of panic in front of too many choices and fear of commitment to any one of them is sadly widespread. For possibility-driven despairers, life is scattered, dissipated. No center holds, no counterweight of necessity draws their spinning wheels down to earth where they can begin to make contact and move forward. In English, the adjective "desperate" captures much of the feeling tone of this experience.

Closest to the standard English connotations of the word "despair" are the experiences at the other ends of Kierkegaard's polarities — the despairs of finitude and of necessity. Where the despair of infinity flies off into a realm of fantasy, the opposite despair resists fantasy altogether, resists the imaginal, resists anything beyond the routine, prosaic, pragmatic details of daily experience. ("Just the facts, ma'am, just the facts.") To conform to the crowd is the sole ambition. The despair of finitude bogs itself down in conventionality.

The despair of necessity also feels bogged down, boxed in — not by routines and conventions, but by the sense that everything is foreordained and futile, unchanging and unchangeable. When Isabel sinks into lassitude, slowly gaining weight because she cannot summon the energy for any activity other than eating and sleeping, she resigns herself to her slow self-destruction: "This seemed as inevitable as the color of my hair," she sighs. When Celie looks at the world around her and comments on "how flat it look to me," she articulates the vision of one who is so oppressed by what seems inevitable that she is unable to see any leaven of possibility. A person who despairs because of too much necessity is one who cannot or will not believe in the opening up of fresh avenues leading out of the flatness of present frustrations and futility. Diametrically opposite from the paralysis of overchoice, this despair suffers the debilitation of "under-choice" and the impotence of too little control over its own existence.

When Kierkegaard talks about the four key forms of despair which originate in an imbalance within the polarities of human selfhood, he finds the sufferers' consciousness of their condition to be largely irrelevant. Indeed, he notes that a certain degree of unconsciousness is characteristic in each case. The despairs of infinity and possibility attempt to evade the demands of genuine self-awareness by taking flights into the fantastic, into the seductive realm of never-to-be-actualized potential. The despair of finitude undertakes its evasion of awareness through attempting to conform with the crowd. The despair of necessity anaesthetizes the pains of struggling against present obstacles in the path of self-realization by resigning itself to a foregone conclusion of defeat. In all these instances, the fact that a person is unconscious of being in despair merely testifies to the virulent subtlety of the dis-ease which lies at the heart of the fragmented self.

Conscious Despair

It is possible to live a whole lifetime in one or more of the above forms of unconscious despair. However, Kierkegaard strongly contends that to do so is to condemn ourselves to a fragile existence. Even if we think that we are happy, such happiness skates on the brink of serious disillusionment. If contentment is purchased at the price of never examining our lives too carefully, then we are vulnerable indeed! What happens when some tragedy forces us to look at ourselves and the ways we are living? What happens to Isabel when her father dies and destroys the complacency of the dutiful-daughter role she has so self-protectively assumed? The prospect of such stark awakening haunts our lives at every moment, though we may attempt to ignore it in our frenzied pursuit of possibility or our wearied capitulation to the necessary. As Kierkegaard observes, we can live in self-deception and in various evasive tactics for a long time — perhaps for a lifetime. But perhaps (and it is very likely), the sad moment will come when the whole house of cards will fall fluttering down around our feet. . . .

When it does, if it does, we will have entered a new level of "potentiation" — a new level of awareness. We will have become conscious of our despair. Kierkegaard divides the level of conscious despairing into two principal varieties: the despair of weakness or "not willing to be oneself," and the despair of defiance or "willing to be oneself."

Despairs of Weakness

The character Isabel from Mary Gordon's *Final Payments* provides a perfect example for this kind of despair which marks an initial and painful step into self-awareness. Her comment on her father's burial is telling: "It was the end of my life as well.

After they lowered his body, I would have to invent an existence for myself" (10). From the time of his first stroke until the day of his funeral, her existence is so clear, if so caught up in the unconscious despair of necessity. The requirements of caring for an invalid give her certainty and purpose; they "[encase her] in meaning like crystal" (12). She never has to occupy herself with who she is or what she wants out of life, because her days are defined by the schedule of attending to someone else's needs. Consequently, the freedom to define her new life makes her dizzy. Her universe grows suddenly "gravityless," "airy" with an excess of possibility. She shrinks from having to "invent" a new existence. In Kierkegaard's language, she feels too weak for the task. She does not have the will to be herself.

Kierkegaard refers to this weak-willed condition as a "womanly" despair. In the late twentieth century, it is perhaps tempting to level charges of sexism at him for this designation. Clearly, there are occasions when such charges would be in order; Kierkegaard is no women's liberationist, either in his life or his writings. However, the sad truth remains that many women do get caught in the trap of looking to something or someone outside ourselves to approve of us, to give us a sense of our own meaning and value. Many of the young women college students I talk with still tend to care more about what their parents or boyfriends think about them than about what they think of themselves. Whether such a tendency is the exclusive province of women or not; whether it issues from a conditioned response to sexist socialization or from an inherent aptitude for the values of relationship over those of autonomy — these are intriguing but peripheral debates at this juncture. What is more central for the present discussion is that Kierkegaard, in many ways so remote from late-twentieth century feminism, is nevertheless so astute in his description of the "womanly" despair which arises from a "fear of success" and an "ethic of care" run riot.[7]

The despair of weakness has its own gradations or levels of potentiation. The first is that of *despair over something earthly*. Isabel, once again, provides a pertinent illustration. Moving back into the world after the isolated years of caring for her father, she finds herself poignantly out of touch. At a Community Center function, the extent of her alienation becomes apparent: "I remembered that I had not danced in eleven years, and that the last dance I had done was the twist. I could not possibly do that here." Tears of loneliness and hot embarrassment send her rushing from the room, even as the silliness of their provocation strikes her: "What could I say? 'I'm crying because I don't know any of the dances'? It was absurd" (116).

So, indeed, does much despair at this level have a dimension of "absurdity" in its provocation. I recall reading somewhere the comment of a woman government official who acknowledged that she could cope with fiscal and political crises with great equanimity, but be thrown into a panic of utter desperation at the discovery of a run in her hose on her way out the door to a campaign function. The "something earthly" which occasions our despair at this level can appear to us, even in the moment, as ridiculous. Nevertheless, it is sufficient to deplete our coping resources; we lose the will to go on, we would just as soon give up on our life altogether — an extreme, but ever-so-familiar reaction to a run in the hose or not knowing the right dances.

What makes this kind of reaction even more understandable is that despair rarely remains at the restricted gradation of being over "something earthly." Rather, it sinks by a gravity all its own to ever deeper and more encompassing levels, acting all the way down as a kind of emotional magnet. Once one "earthly" object has entered its force field, despair seems to open up to attract more and more objects into itself. First Isabel feels despair over not knowing any dances; then she despairs because she has no place to run and hide, having sold the house where she lived with her father during his increasing infirmity. Then she despairs because he is dead, and she is alone, and the emptiness of her life threatens to suck her into a vortex in which she will whirl dizzyingly around and around with no possibility of escape. Shortly after sobbing over her ignorance of the new dances, she finds herself "once more . . . looking down at my life from that height" (116). Her despair over something earthly spreads out to encompass a *"despair over the earthly in toto."*

Nor does the spread of despairing stop even here. A nagging discontent goads the despairer into realizing that it is not so much her world that is finally at fault, but rather her self. The example which Kierkegaard provides in *The Sickness Unto Death* is of a young girl who has lost her lover; the description applies to Isabel's loss of her father as well. Initially, Kierkegaard writes, "A young girl is in despair over love, and so she despairs over her lover because he died or because he was unfaithful to her." But, he continues:

> No, she is in despair over herself. This self of hers, which, if it had become "his" beloved, she would have been rid of in the most blissful way, . . . this self is now a torment to her when it has to be a self without "him"; this self which would have been to her riches . . . has now become to her a loathsome void (152–153).

Isabel's self is a "loathsome void" when her father's death leaves her without a crystalline definition of roles and responsibilities to fill and justify her existence: "I hated my own uncertainty," she writes, "my lack of authority, my concern for what people thought and felt about me" (90). In this one line, she sums up what Kierkegaard defines as the next level of potentiation for the despair of weakness — namely, "*despair over oneself for taking the earthly too much to heart*" (195–196).

At this level, the "despair of weakness" (of "not willing to be oneself") has become what Kierkegaard aptly labels a "despair *over* weakness." The person in despair compounds her problem by hating herself for being so weak as to succumb to despairing. In turn, she compounds this very self-hatred by a common, if perverse, move toward increased "introversion." While companionship might take the sufferer out of her despair, instead a self-chosen isolation drives her deeper and deeper into it. In solitude, she can uninterruptedly nurse the wound of her affliction. The silent isolation into which both Isabel and Celie sink at the nadir of their despairing gives pointed witness to the reality, and the peril, of such "introverting" tendencies.

In one of the flashes of insight which makes Kierkegaard's mirror of human experience so revealing, he notes how the self-loathing of an introverted despair over weakness actually constitutes a form of pride. The person in despair, however, is reluctant to acknowledge this. He (even though this is a "womanly" despair, Kierkegaard writes of it in the masculine) tells himself "that it could not possibly be pride, for it was in fact precisely over his weakness that he was in despair — just as if it were not pride which attached such prodigious weight to weakness, just as if it were not because he wanted to be proud of himself that he could not endure the consciousness of weakness" (198–199). There is a startling truth in this observation. Self-loathing does display a form of self-centeredness, a preoccupation with the self and its weaknesses (even if the customary notion of pride focuses on the self and its strengths). Kierkegaard is pointing here to a paradox: while despair emerges out of a reluctance to take responsibility for oneself, an obsessive concern with self can land one in despair equally well (and the two are not, after all, terribly far-removed from each other).

This paradox appears in the very labels Kierkegaard has chosen for his two principal varieties of conscious despairing: the despair of weakness or "not willing to be oneself" is complemented by the despair of defiance or "willing to be oneself." We have seen the former manifest itself as *despair over something earthly, despair over the earthly in toto,* and *despair over the self for taking the earthly too much to heart.* Before moving on to see how the latter ("willful" despair) manifests its own varying levels and gradations, we would do well to pause a moment and consider precisely what it is that Kierkegaard means by "being oneself" — whether one does or does not will so to be.

Kierkegaard's presuppositions about selfhood are religiously colored, even in his phenomenology of the levels of despair experienced by a "humanist" self. As we noted earlier, in his lexicon the word "despair" refers to a "two-ness" or "dividedness" in the human spirit which forces our opposing inner poles of infinity and finitude, possibility and necessity, into perpetual disequilibrium. Yet, Kierkegaard assumes that such disequilibrium is neither the state in which human beings were created, nor the end for which we were destined. Rather, we sprang from our creator's hand whole and harmonious; we were intended for the deep-rooted happiness which only such harmony can sustain. We have fundamentally distorted the balance of right relationships within our own spirits by pulling away from the one right relationship which could keep the whole in equi-librated order. Only by emptying out our own pretensions to self-ordering and becoming "transparent" to the Power which placed us and holds us in being can we be healed of the divisive-ness which constitutes the dis-ease of despair. Thus, to become *fully a self*, for Kierkegaard, is quite the opposite of becoming *full of oneself*. To become fully a self is to become the individual that one was created to be, actualizing one's possibilities while recognizing the limitations of one's givenness — all in humble accord with the Power who is ultimately the source of both. The problem with the despair of weakness is that it wants to put the responsibility for defining and actualizing the self onto some other human person (as Isabel initially wants to do with her father; as Celie at several points wants to do with Shug). In contrast, the problem with the despair of defiance is that it wants to claim sole responsibility for self-actualization, without regard to limitations or contributions given to the self by other persons or by the "positing Power" of God.

Despairs of Defiance

Let us turn, then, to look at Kierkegaard's depictions of the despairs of defiance. Whereas the weakness of "not willing to be oneself" was considered "womanly," the defiance of willing to be oneself all by oneself is (predictably) labeled a "manly" despair. As Kierkegaard describes him, the "manly" despairer "wills . . . to refashion . . . [his 'self'] in order to get out of it . . . a self such as he wants to have." The stress is upon the wants — however selfish, however unrealistic — of the individual. "He is not willing to attire himself in himself, nor to see his task in the self given him; [but rather] he wills to construct it himself" (196). With a wild pretense of godlikeness, he would begin not "with the beginning but 'in the beginning'," aiming to fabricate himself *ex nihilo*. Aptly enough, in Kierkegaard's analysis, as down through the Christian tradition, despair keeps close com-pany with presumption.

It is less easy to find examples of presumptuous and defiant despairing in the stories of Isabel and Celie, unless we look to the male characters in those stories whom we have not yet spent much time exploring.[8] Rather than attempt to unravel a whole new set of story lines from *Final Payments* and *The Color Purple*, let us turn instead to creating our own composite portrait of a willful despairer. In deference to Kierkegaard's categories, I will describe this despairer in masculine language, but will leave it an open question whether or not women are as immune to this affliction as he might have it.

Let us imagine a man who has a job which he enjoys, at which he would like to succeed. His desires for success, however, sometimes lead him to destructive extremes. Eager for the approval of his superiors, he agrees to every task which they propose. As a result, he loses control over his time. He is forced to take work home with him in the evenings, staying up later than he knows is healthy for him, rising early in the mornings before his body is adequately refreshed. He grows tense and short-tempered with his family and friends, all the while he struggles to remain gracious in all his official encounters. The duality of this existence creates an additional strain on him. Pressures mount. The list of items to which he must attend seems to stretch longer and longer. With so many commitments, he eventually becomes unable to fulfill any one of them to his satisfaction. No sooner has he started work on one project than panic overtakes him at the thought of the three other ones which he should be tackling instead. So he shifts his focus, only to be attacked by guilt and indecision once again. The work, and the frustrations, pile ever higher. At length, one day, something snaps. Paralyzed, he sits and watches in a kind of horrified bewitchment as the deadlines for finishing his appointed tasks creep ever nearer and he feels incapacitated to move forward to meet them. He can merely shake his head numbly. He has failed. He is worthless. He finds himself in despair.

The marks of this particular form of defiant despairing are easy to discern. Despite all the limits that come with being human, including basic bodily needs for rest and recreation, this man strives toward some superhuman ideal. He actively wills to be a certain kind of person — self-sufficient, indefatigable, omnicompetent — and he falls into bitter recriminations when this goal turns out to be unrealizable. Such "willing to be a self," however, is wrong on two counts. First, it takes its own chosen (and inflated) goals with narcissistic seriousness, "bestow[ing] upon its undertakings infinite interest and importance" (202). Second, it is so intent on self-creation that it refuses to acknowledge any kind of relatedness to sources or sustenance outside itself.

Here again, Kierkegaard's mirror of human foibles is illuminating. Referring to a defiant despairer who has backed himself into a corner with his unrealistic goals and his desperate striving for utter self-sufficiency, Kierkegaard explains: "It is not quite so true after all when people say that 'it is a matter of course that a sufferer would be so glad to be helped, if only somebody would help him.'" Indeed, the contrary is more likely the case. "A sufferer has one or more ways in which he would be glad to be helped. If he is helped thus, he is willing to be helped" (205). If we can be helped on our own terms, well and good — because at least then we are still in control, still calling the shots and making the decisions. But if "help" means surrendering control or acknowledging that our self-image is faulty and our goals and choices are self-deceived, then fie on anyone who should propose such assistance! Masters of the game "Why Don't You . . . Yes, But" — identified in Eric Berne's clever analysis of *Games People Play* — defiant despairers have a ready answer for why no proposal of help could actually be worth accepting: "Yes [as in, 'Yes, that might be a constructive suggestion in some situations'], But [as in, 'But it would never work for *me*']."[9]

Operating out of his theological presuppositions, Kierkegaard does not limit his critique of the defiant despairer to such refusals of help from other people. Ultimately, in his understanding, the rejection of support and assistance amounts to a refusal of surrender to the Power which created the individual and which alone can restore him or her to healthful equilibrium. Thus, the *"despair which refuses comfort from beyond the self"* — an initial gradation of willful despairing — shows itself to be, at bottom, a *"despair which refuses comfort from the eternal."* In perversity and self-pity, the defiant despairer decides that he would rather have the certainty of the pains he knows so well than surrender to the uncertainty of help from a Source he can neither see nor control. He would rather live with the torments of his willful existence than undergo "the humiliation of having to accept help unconditionally and in any way," especially "the humiliation of becoming nothing in the hand of the Helper for whom all things are possible" (203–205). In Kierkegaard's analysis, this refusal of help — whether from another person or from God — can culminate in a kind of rage. The person strikes up against some feature of her existence which is the source of misery. Perhaps, like Isabel, she feels alone, abandoned, grief-stricken; perhaps, like Celie, she is a victim of abuse. If the person descends to the level which Kierkegaard identifies as "demoniac despair," she chooses to focus all her passion on her particular torment, such that it gradually comes to define her very reason for being. With it, she can lay claim to being "the one [person] in the whole of existence who is the most unjustly treated," whereas without it, she would be ordinary, lackluster, lost. Rather than hope, then, for any possible improvement in her situation, the person chooses to hold onto misery with a fierce determination. The demoniac despairer "will not hear about what comfort eternity has" to offer, because this comfort would take away the very cornerstone of her identity as angry victim (205–207). Such a person prefers *despair which rages against the eternal* as the source of bitter victimization to trust which looks to the eternal as the potential source of comfort and healing.

Yet the two — rage and trust — bear a markedly close affinity to one another. In degree of passionateness, Kierkegaard would say, they are equivalent. To shake one's fist in prophetic fury against injustice is at least to avow a serious stake in the right ordering of reality; it is to cry out, even in anguish, "I *care!*" Rage shatters apathy — as it did for both Isabel and Celie (neither of whom lingers at the level of demoniac despairing, being propelled into epiphany by their anger rather than compelled into obsessive preoccupation with it). It is not altogether coincidental that Luther counseled as remedy for despair, "Get downright angry!"[10] Rage is "spirited"; it is impassioned and concerned. Because of its intensity of spirit, the rage of the "humanist self" whose desires for justice and fulfillment have been thwarted shades very close to the despair of a "theological self" who is conscious of existing perennially in the difficult and demanding presence of God. The latter consciousness, however, no longer belongs within the phenomenological description of psychological forms of despair. Rather, it breaks into a new dimension — one wherein despair is no longer simply the "sickness" of disequilibration and dis-ease within the self, but, because it is rebellion in the sight of God, must be seen as *sin*.

Before moving to explore this new dimension, however, I must sound a note of caution. There is something dangerously deceptive in the preceding rehearsal of Kierkegaard's continuum of phenomenological analysis. It might seem to imply that there are developmental stages of despair through which every sufferer will or should pass. Such an implication, however, is misleading on three counts.

First, very few individuals — according to Kierkegaard — ever truly own up to the seriousness of their condition in such a way as to evoke the passion of raging defiance. Most of us, most of the time, persist in a minimal and passive degree of awareness of our predicament. Our despair remains at a rudimentary level; we sigh over the anticipated failure of health, wealth, or relationship, without ever sighing over the self of ours which is more fundamentally at fault for pinning so much hope on these transient values. ("It is always despair," Kierkegaard writes, "to have one's life dependent upon that which may pass away."[11]) Not every despairer will pass from this rudimentary level to the deeper and more conscious levels of Kierkegaard's continuum. No inherent, developmental dynamism will move us to more "potentiated" levels of despairing unless we become sufficiently self-aware to *will* ourselves so to move.

The second count on which the implications of a continuum describing gradations of despair may be misleading has to do with the possible assumption that more potentiated forms of despair are somehow "better." True, they represent growth into greater degrees of self-awareness which may bring us to a greater lucidity about the real source of our problems and about the need to turn to a source of healing outside ourselves. However, such a turn is in no way an inevitable outcome of deep levels of despairing. It is quite possible that we may come to suffer ever more self-consciously and acutely, only to remain stuck in such agony. Or, conversely, it is also possible that we may not require the depths of intense and "demoniac" despair before we recognize the gravity of our condition and turn in humility to seek healing assistance from "the Helper to whom all things are possible." Genuine healing may occur at any level of despair — or it may elude at every point. The decisive factor is our readiness to surrender — a readiness which may be approached by developing intensities of our problem, but which can never be guaranteed.

The necessity for "surrender" raises the third count on which developmental implications about despair necessitate caution. In Kierkegaard's understanding, "surrender" is a fundamentally religious act. In accordance with his theological presuppositions, he sees the recovery of hopeful and harmonious personal wholeness to be possible only through "transparent" — which is to say, "trustful" — grounding in the Power which placed and holds the self in being. Despair *at every level* is traceable to a breach in relationship with this Power. Thus, at every level, despair has a religious root. To assume from the diagram outlining Kierkegaard's gradations of despair, from the headings within this chapter, or from the two-part division of *The Sickness Unto Death* that a person moves from elemental forms of despair which are purely psychological into an intensified level at which they "become" theological would be a serious oversimplification. The relationship which Kierkegaard posits between despair as *Stemning* or "mood" and despair as "sin" is highly paradoxical. We will occupy ourselves in detail with this paradoxical relationship as we turn now to a fuller exploration of the theology of despair as found in *The Sickness Unto Death*, "Part Second: Despair Is Sin."

Theology of Despair

In his journal for the year 1848, Kierkegaard confides: "The despairing person complains about despair and does not hear that it is — a self-accusation."[12] In fact, it is one of the most serious self-accusations imaginable. "Have you considered what it is to despair?" Kierkegaard demands in one of his religious discourses. "Alas, it is to deny that God is love! ... One who despairs . . . abandons God."[13] To complain about despair is to confess to something grievously wrong in one's God-relationship. As with Luther, it is to confess to the ego-ridden failure to love God with all one's heart, soul, mind, and strength. As with Aquinas and others in the Christian tradition, it is to confess to the unforgivable "Sin against the Holy Ghost" (262).

This assessment of the sinful severity of despair raises a number of questions. In particular, it calls for some clarity of definition: what is the distinctive nature of the despair which is defined to be sin? How does this "theological" despair relate to the "mood" of despair discussed in the preceding phenomenology? We have suggested that the relationship involved is a "paradoxical" one; now we need to examine that paradox in some detail.

Kierkegaard gives a concise but cryptic definition of despair as sin (his syntax can, indeed, be daunting):

> Sin is this: *before God, or with the conception of God, to be in despair at not willing to be oneself, or to be in despair at willing to be oneself.* Thus sin is potentiated weakness or potentiated defiance: sin is the potentiation of despair (208).

According to this definition, sin is despair raised to a higher intensity by virtue of the fact that it occurs in the sight of God. What is, therefore, a human problem of defective or disordered will — evidenced in the "womanly" yearning to be rid of the burden of self-definition or the "manly" eagerness to define the self in superhuman terms — becomes a theological problem when God enters the picture: because the self that one "does not will to be" is a gift of divine creation; and the self that one "wills to be" all by oneself rejects the help of divine providence.

As in his phenomenology, so in his theological analysis Kierkegaard elaborates a continuum of experiences. "Despair as sin" manifests itself on three levels:

DESPAIR WHICH IS CONSCIOUS
OF BEING BEFORE GOD
|
Despair Over One's Sin
|
Despair of the Forgiveness of Sin
|
Despair Which Abandons Christianity as False

As with the psychological levels, these forms follow one another in degrees of increasing volition — from "weak" and defensive evasion of the gospel of forgiveness, to "defiant" and offensive attack on the truthfulness of the gospel itself. As the forms grow more volitional on their way down the continuum, they simultaneously grow more intense and more severe.

However, we must be cautious in dealing with the theological continuum, just as we had to observe certain closing cautions in discussing the continuum of phenomenological analysis. There is a paradoxical sense in which "worse" or "more severe" in Kierkegaard's lexicon can actually mean "better": insofar as despair is a "dialectical" sickness, an increase in intensity may move it closer to healing. After all, the more acutely something hurts me, the less likely I am to discount it and the more likely I am to seek help for my condition.

At the same time, however, despair of any degree of intensity before God is equally deserving of damnation, as Kierkegaard declaims in the following admonition:

> Eternity asks of . . . every individual . . . only one question, whether thou hast lived in despair or not, whether thou wast in despair in such a way that thou didst not know thou wast in despair, or in such a way that thou didst hiddenly carry this sickness in thine inward parts as thy gnawing secret, . . . or in such a way that thou, a horror to others, didst rave in despair. And if so, if thou hast lived in despair . . . , then for thee all is lost, eternity knows thee not, . . . or (even more dreadful) it knows thee as thou art known, it puts thee under arrest by thyself in despair (160–161).

Kierkegaard is warning here that once we are separated from God, degrees and expressions of our separation make no ultimate difference. As with Luther (in contrast to the Roman Catholic tradition of genealogies and gradations), Sin is Sin. Nevertheless, there are differing guises under which the sin of our separation may appear, and it is with the intent of unmasking them that Kierkegaard presents his continuum of analysis.

The Categories of Theological Despair

The first guise of despairing which is explicitly conscious of its God-relationship is *despair over one's sin*. This form of "theological" despair bears a close kinship to the phenomenological "despair over oneself for taking the earthly too much to heart." Both conceal a problem of pride, of preoccupation with self rather than self-surrender. Kierkegaard acknowledges that the world of Romanticism tends to view despair over one's sinful self as expressing a "deep nature"; being "unable to forgive oneself" masquerades as the mark of a pious spirit. To this deception, he counters: Not so! The French have a saying that *qui s'excuse, s'accuse* (the person who makes excuses for himself is thereby accusing himself). Kierkegaard would modify that saying to read *qui s'accuse, s'accuse*: the person who is intent on accusing herself of some personal deficiency is thereby in fact accusing herself of spending too much time massaging her personal foibles. In the final analysis, despair over one's short-comings "is selfish . . . because it is self-love which would like to be proud of itself, like to be without sin." The Romantic ravings of the sinner who "never can forgive" the self are thus "pretty nearly the opposite of penitent contrition which prays to God for forgiveness" (240–243). Thus, despair over one's sin is a first guise in which "potentiated," theological despairing appears: standing "before God," it would rather fixate on its own small nature than look beyond itself to the possibilities of healing from the grandeur of the divine.

The second guise of theological despair is closely related. *Despair of forgiveness* differs from *despair over sin* only in the nuancing of its object and the degree of its willfulness. Kierkegaard plays on the fact that the word "despair" operates with a variety of following prepositions.[14] We despair *over* that which lands us in despair: Isabel despairs over her father's death and her new free-floating loneliness; Celie despairs over the loss of the two loves of her life, Nettie and Shug. In contrast to this, we despair *of* that which we think would heal our distress, if only it would happen: Isabel despairs of being able to love anyone ever again, in the face of the threat of mortality; Celie despairs of Shug's ever coming back to her. While none of the "old moralists" of the Christian tradition see fit to make this distinc-tion, for Kierkegaard it is important. Despairing not just *over* sin but *of* forgiveness signifies an intensified awareness of the "object" of despair, of the end in which true healing lies. Consequently, to turn away from this end is to show an even greater willfulness and perversity. It is as if God held out to me the possibility of becoming whole and healthy — and I looked squarely at the offer and shook my head, "no." This, says Kierkegaard, is the equivalent of "picking a quarrel with God." Granted, my refusal to believe in the possibility of healing and forgiveness at least shows that I recognize the radicality of such an offer. However, it also shows that I would rather rely on my own fallible judgment that something is "too good to be true" than surrender my judgment to embrace in faith that the gospel means the "too good" has become Truth indeed.

In the third guise or level of expressly sinful despairing, I not only "pick a quarrel with God" through not daring to believe that forgiveness is possible. Even more, I launch a full-scale spiritual offensive. Directly facing the good news of Christianity that God is infinitely concerned with human happiness and that loving forgiveness is available to heal the pains of a broken spirit, I actively deny that such is true. I take offense at the Christ; I find it intolerably absurd that the Almighty, the Eternal should have deigned to exist in human flesh at a particular point in history. I find it presumptuous and ridiculous to believe that the Ultimate in being, meaning, and value should care about *me*. And so I manifest the most serious potentiation of despair on Kierkegaard's continuum: the *abandonment of Christianity as false*. This abandonment, this rejection constitutes "the sin against the Holy Ghost" (213, 262). It constitutes a breach with faith. Because sin (for Kierkegaard, as for Luther) has far more to do with a failure of faith than with a deficiency of virtue, the ultimate form of sin is this potentiation of despair — this refusal to believe and trust in the only Power which could bring the willful, warring dualities of the self back into harmonious accord.

The Relationship of Theological and Phenomenological Categories of Despair

We have thus answered the first question pertinent to our exploration of Kierkegaard's theology of despair: What is the distinctive nature of the despair which he defines to be sin? His answer: it is despair in the presence of God; specifically, it is despair over sin, despair of forgiveness, and final rejection of Christian truth. Beyond this, a second question sounds: How does "theological" despair, so defined, relate to the "mood" of despair discussed in Part First of *The Sickness Unto Death* and in the first section of this chapter? At first blush, the answer to this second question appears a simple one. Theological despair seems to be distinguished by the nature of the objects with which it is concerned. The phenomenologically-analyzed "mood" despairs over a deceased father and departed friends; the theological affliction despairs over sin and the presumed impossibility of forgiveness. Despair becomes theological when it intends a theological object. There is certainly comfort in this answer: if the distinction is truly "object-specific," then as long as I am despairing over something other than the providence of God, I am off the hook of having to understand my despair as sin.

Unfortunately, however, matters are not quite so simple. The relationship between psychological and theological despair is far more paradoxical. On the one hand, the two classes of despair *are* experientially indistinguishable. To the sufferer, the despair over sin "feels" no different from a despair over the self for taking the earthly too much to heart; what differentiates one from the other does have more to do with the "external" object than with the internal dynamics of the experience. "To be a sinner *in the strictest sense*," Kierkegaard specifies, I must be vividly aware of my existence before God (212 and 232, my emphasis). Without an awareness of that object, my experience scarcely deserves the dignity that would be conferred upon it by theological categories.

On the other hand, however — and this is where the paradox emerges — the full extent of sin is not limited to "sin in the strictest sense." As we read earlier, Kierkegaard finds *all* forms of despair to be damning: "whether thou wast in despair in such a way that thou didst not know thou wast in despair," whether the awareness of existing before God has been present or not (160–161). Consequently, the simple object-specific view of the relation between mood and sin will not finally hold. Even those forms of despair which do not expressly intend a theological object stand thereby convicted of "the sin of . . . the despairing

105

unawareness of God, unawareness of existing before God [which means being] 'without God in the world.'"[15] Whether I own up to it or not, I am always in God's providential care. Thus, to despair over *any* object, theological or otherwise, is to demonstrate doubts in that providence — doubts which exemplify my estrangement from God, which is Kierkegaard's definition of sin.

This paradoxical understanding of the relationship between despair as sin and despair as mood is distinctive to Kierkegaard and Luther within the Christian tradition. For Thomas Aquinas, as we have seen, the relationship is more straightforward: sins are acts contrary to virtue; according to his criteria, despair is a sin when it is volitional, when it eludes the control of "right reason," and when it deliberately rejects the "object" of the "divine good." For Kierkegaard and Luther, however, sin is not so much an act contrary to virtue as it is a condition contrary to faith. The sin of "unfaith" — of the inability to trust God in total self-surrender — describes the situation of a self so alienated from its intended wholeness that it is unable to exercise either its will or its reason aright. Because we are sinners, because we are alienated from God, we are prey to moods of despair which wash over us irrationally and involuntarily — and we are culpable for them just as much as we are culpable for the more seemingly deliberate acts of despair which reject the "divine good" of grace, forgiveness, or hope. Experiences of despair — regardless of their object, their phenomenology, their degree of consciousness or volitional consent — make evident our condition of Sin (in the singular). For Kierkegaard, as for Luther, this is far more significant than whether or not such experiences constitute sins (in the plural) as specific acts of vice. Despair of possibility or necessity; despair over something earthly or over the earthly *in toto*; weak or defiant despair over the self — all these moods emerge out of and testify to a serious brokenness in human existence. They are all, therefore, implicated in sinfulness, even though their intentionality may not be theological "in the strictest sense." Phenomenological and theological categories thus interpenetrate in a paradoxical fashion: a despairing mood may not be, in the strictest sense, *a* sin; nonetheless, it gives evidence, in the severest sense, of Sin itself.

Despair and Healing

Where despair is always evidence of an underlying state of Sin, certain implications for its healing arise. The most important of these is that healing is always a matter of grace. Just as Christian theology teaches us that we do not redeem ourselves from sinfulness, so Kierkegaard's phenomenology and theology alike insist that we do not remedy our own despair. This insistence may be discouraging if we are expecting *The Sickness Unto Death* to provide us with a self-help manual complete with "how-to's" for the conquest of despairing. However, Kierkgaard's insights in this regard have ultimately encouraging potential. Above all, they can help to relieve the burden of self-preoccupation which perpetuates despair, assuring us that healing graces attend us beyond the confines of our own limited abilities.

The first passage of *The Sickness Unto Death* in which Kierkegaard writes at any length about healing appears in his discussion of the unconscious despair of unequilibrated necessity. Here he is quite explicit: *Possibility*, he insists, is "the only saving remedy" (172). Even though at this point he is still dealing with the "mood" of despair experienced by a "humanist" self, his reference is not simply to human possibilities. In fact, he is adamant in maintaining that reliance on our personal achievements and foresight alone virtually condemns us to remaining in a desperate condition. According to his convictions, however, our limited possibilities do not exhaust reality. As he exhorts himself in a crucial journal entry from May of 1848:

> Just because I do not see any way out, I must not for an instant be so presumptuous as to say that there could be no way out for God. For this is despair and presumption, to confound one's bit of imagination with the possibility God disposes of.[16]

Again, Kierkegaard echoes the wisdom of the "old moralists" of the Christian tradition: despair and presumption are indeed close kin. Both refuse to believe that there could be any way out of current difficulties — simply because the self, in its present frustrations, is unable to foresee one.

107

In opposition to the despair of necessity which arises out of presumptuous reliance on one's own "bit of imagination," Kierkegaard counsels the healing discipline of humility. The believer — his contrast figure to the person in despair — "leaves it wholly to God how he is to be helped, but believes that for God all things are possible" (172). Reiterating this theme with regard to the despairs of defiance, Kierkegaard professes that healing requires the "humiliation of having to accept help unconditionally and in any way, the humiliation of becoming nothing in the hand of the Helper for whom all things are possible" (205). The conquest of despair thus demands a dual sacrifice: we must surrender the seductive certainty of our intellect which can envision no release from a situation, in deference to the uncertainty of trust in God's unforeseeable possibilities; and we must renounce the desires of our will to triumph self-sufficiently over all obstacles, in deference to the need to acknowledge our own limitations and dependency. If we can overcome our pride and presumption sufficiently to believe that grace-filled possibilities await us beyond the confines of our current imagining, then we are well on our way to emerging from despair into wholeness and hope.

This prescription for healing sounds very similar to some of Luther's recommendations, about which we earlier cited Roland Bainton's comment: they are "in a way prescribing faith as a cure for the lack of faith."[17] The faith at issue, however, is not assent to particular doctrines; rather, it is a kind of steady, at times doggedly determined, trust — a willingness to wait for the flowering of things in their own due season, apart from the demands and machinations of our own "bit of imagination." In fact, this kind of faith bears a resemblance to the patient discernment which Evagrius Ponticus counseled. It is tenacity in the midst of struggle, persistent loyalty in the very thick of trials and doubts. Paradoxically, it is at one and the same time a supreme act of will and a supreme renunciation of will: it insists that although I can see no way out of this situation, nevertheless, I will trust.

Despite their similar visions of despair as "unfaith" for which a tenacious trust is the sovereign cure, Kierkegaard and Luther do demonstrate a significant difference in their theologies of healing. For both theologians, because despair is sin, the source of its redemption/remediation must lie in grace. Luther, however, pays much more attention than does Kierkegaard to the potential mediation of grace through earthly measures. He recommends food, drink, companionship, rest, and recreation as agencies through which the anguish of despair can be assuaged. God's creation is good, Luther is affirming. Like Shug talking to Celie ("God love all them feelings. That's some of the best stuff God did" [178]), so Luther entreats us: "Be merry, both inwardly in Christ and outwardly in his gifts and the good things of life."[18] In such merriment, we will find — to our relief and our rejoicing — that God's creation mediates a grace sufficient to drive away at least some of the pains of our despairing.

In marked contrast to this Lutheran position, Kierkegaard ultimately neglects any salutary mediation of grace apart from the explicitly Christian forgiveness of sin. Throughout the first part of *The Sickness Unto Death*, he makes only one passing reference to a non-theological mode of healing. With regard to the despair of necessity, he observes that "sometimes the inventiveness of a human imagination suffices to procure possibility" (172). This type of mediation is sorely limited, however. In fact, it is more harmful than helpful insofar as it alleviates pain and numbs the sufferer's awareness of the deeper sickness underlying his despairing (alienated, sinful) condition. In Kierkegaard's judgment, to rely solely on humanly-procured possibilities in a situation of despair is like taking stimulants for a depressive condition which was itself induced by a prior drug dependency. The attempted cure actually compounds the problem: it introduces a new drug into an already addicted organism, and it masks the real malady such that the search for an appropriate cure is dangerously deferred. The person afflicted with despair is already overly dependent on a presumption of self-sufficiency and the search for human palliatives is a symptom of that presumptuousness rather than a step toward the necessary humility of healing. For Kierkegaard, the broken bond between the human self and the Power which created it underlies and intensifies all other forms of despairing; thus, the healing of the latter cannot fully and satisfactorily occur unless the former is treated. It is the forgiveness of sin which triumphs over this underlying brokenness and offers the ultimate healing. Consequently, in Kierkegaard's theological perspective, no other mediation of grace is sufficiently salutary to merit attention.

Concluding Critical Postscript

Kierkegaard's perspective on healing, distinctive as it is, raises at least as many questions as it answers. First among these is the matter of its divergence from Luther on the role of earthly mediations of grace in the treatment of despair. Within the framework of Christian teaching, we need to ponder whether Kierkegaard's position does full justice to the doctrines of creation and incarnation. Is there a denial of the earthly, the bodily, the materially human at work in Kierkegaard which is antithetical to the ecological and social concerns of the present day?

A second critical question arises out of the Christocentric focus to his diagnosis and prescription for the healing of theological despair. The ultimate sin on his continuum of "Despair That Is Conscious of Being Before God" stands as "the abandonment of Christianity as false." Correlatively, the ultimate healing comes through accepting as true that, in Christ, sin is forgiven. "There has lived no one and there lives no one outside of Christendom, who is not in despair," he sweepingly asserts, "and no one in Christendom, unless he be a true Christian" (155). Of despair as the sickness unto death, he adds: "To be sharply observant of this sickness constitutes the Christian's advantage over the natural man," and "to be healed is the Christian's bliss" (148). The critical question which emerges from such claims concerns the matter of pluralism: Is it true that only Christian's can be healed of despair? What are the meanings and implications of such a claim in the multi-religious context of the late twentieth century?

A third and final critical question emerges out of a different kind of "one-sidedness" in Kierkegaard's discussions of healing. To counter the pains of despair, he counsels humility: the humility to accept help unconditionally, the humility to believe in forgiveness, the humility to surrender my self-reliance to the trust that God's possibilities outdistance my own. However valuable this spiritual direction may be, it does seem to focus heavily on the despairs of defiance and willfulness. What, then, of the despairs of weakness? Having given such a perceptive diagnosis of what he calls the "womanly" despairs, Kierkegaard seems to pay them less heed in his prescription of healing. For the despair of one who is "not willing to be a self," the recommendations of humility and self-surrender seem ill-advised. In an age sensitized by feminist concerns, keenly aware that sin consists in self-abnegation as well as in overweening self-promotion, we would do well to ask the question for which Kierkegaard's fine analysis has prepared us: How is it that the distinctive despair of weakness may meet with healing?

In *The Sickness Unto Death*, Kierkegaard paints a portrait of human despairing which is psychologically and theologically perceptive, and occasionally even startling in the mirror it holds up to our experience. Because it is a provocative portrait, it raises a number of questions for us to consider further in shaping a theology of despair which is responsive to concerns of the late twentieth century (see Chapter Five). Because it is a comprehensive portrait, it also sets the standard for carrying out a systematic phenomenological exploration of despair as a dimension of human experience in the modern world (our task for Chapter Four). Kierkegaard's meticulously thorough analysis of the multiple forms of "the sickness unto death" demonstrates a remarkable degree of psychological penetration, and his attempt to trace the roots of the problem to a fundamental brokenness in human nature recovers theological dimensions of understanding which, after Burton, went neglected for nearly two hundred years. As phenomenology and theology, Kierkegaard's writings from the nineteenth century form a crucial link between the present day and the heritage of the Christian tradition. A capstone for generations of wisdom from the "old moralists" of Christianity, his analysis also stands as a cornerstone for contemporary, constructive reflections.

CHAPTER 4

Contemporary Phenomenology: Can I Help My Despairing?

Thus far, we have looked at despair through a number of different lenses: the stories of Isabel and Celie, the writings of the "old moralists" of the Christian tradition, and the efforts of Søren Kierkegaard to analyze the phenomenological expressions and theological implications of a malaise so serious that he calls it "the sickness unto death." These various lenses focus on the experience of despair in differing ways, yet they disclose nuances of feeling and flashes of insight which bridge some sixteen hundred years. From the solitary monks of the fourth century, enervated by the silent, searing heat of the noonday sun; to Martin Luther in the sixteenth century, embattled by "waves and blasts" of despondency which cause his limbs to tremble; to Isabel and Celie in the twentieth century, worn down by grief and loneliness to the point where living comes to seem "an awful strain" — human beings have known what it is to despair: to suffer a hope grown dim, to face into the future with dread and discouragement rather than confidence and optimistic conviction.

Each of us has known that experience, too, I warrant. Indeed, I imagine (I hope without presuming too much) that anyone who picks up a book on despair to read does so with a personal agenda lurking somewhere in the background. The questions to be explored are not simply academic ones: What are the characteristic dynamics of the experience of despairing; what sense does it make to speak of despair within the Christian tradition under the rubric of sin? The questions are also profoundly personal: What commonalities can I find with *my* experience of despairing; what descriptions can help me better to identify, what insights can help me better to cope with my own condition? When *I* despair, am *I* guilty of sin?

The principal question for me — academically and personally — can be summarized as an issue of accountability: Am I accountable for my despair; can I fairly be held responsible for it? In the Introduction, I phrased this query in the familiar form: Can I "help it" if I despair? In scholarly discussions of the emotions, this issue is often put in terms of *corrigibility*: How corrigible (or "correctable") is a particular emotion; how amenable is it to rational or volitional control? In the influential tradition of Thomas Aquinas, the answers to such questions provide the criteria for differentiating between despair as an amoral "passion" and despair as an act of vice. Consequently, the question of accountability or corrigibility is an important issue to clarify before returning to the theological concerns with which Kierkegaard left us at the end of Chapter Three.

Can I help it if I am in despair? To tackle this concern directly and systematically entails investigating a series of related matters. First among these is the task of achieving some greater precision about the kind of despair I am experiencing when I pose the question. If I were to ask, "Can I help it if I am in pain?" more than likely a person's first response would be: "Well, that depends. What type of pain do you mean?" Clearly, if I mean the pain that comes from picking up a hot skillet without benefit of potholder, then yes, I can "help it": for one thing, I can drop the skillet; for another, I can take responsibility for not being so careless in the future. I am reminded of the old joke where a patient complains, "Doctor, my back hurts in two places," to which the physician replies — probably while brandishing a rubber chicken — "Well, then, stay out of those places!"

With regard to despair, the point of the above is that there may well be "places" that I can "stay out of " in order to prevent at least certain kinds of despairing. But what kinds — and what places? The corrigibility of despair, or my accountability for it, cannot be adequately determined apart from a *taxonomy* of types (or, as with Kierkegaard, levels) of the experience. Such a taxonomy, in turn, depends upon a variety of issues: the particular provocation (the cause, occasion, and object of my despairing); the "cognitive consorts," or ideas and awarenesses which accompany my experience; and the overall duration of the despair, from episodic to entrenched. As we turn to investigate these issues, we will do well to keep in mind that our guiding concern is not so much curiosity as it is compassion. Academically and personally, we want to discover — for ourselves and for others — not only what can fairly be held accountable for our despair, but also what can helpfully be done for its prevention and healing.

Taxonomy of Despair

Despair exists and operates in a variety of forms, from the relatively superficial and short-lived to the painfully profound and pervasive. In exploring Søren Kierkegaard's phenomenology of despair, we have already seen one way of defining such levels. Twentieth-century students of despair (particularly those who would call themselves "phenomenologists of human emotions") parallel Kierkegaard's insights in a number of striking ways. The following schematic gives a skeletal outline of such parallels:

DURATION	KIERKEGAARD	20th CENTURY	OBJECT
short episodic	Despair over "something earthly"	Despair as a "negative, contending emotion" (Magda Arnold)	specific restricted
	Despair over "the earthly in toto"	Despair as a "generalized emotion" (Robert Solomon)	
entrenched dispositional	Despair over "oneself"	Despair and "moods" (Robert Roberts)	global non-specifiable

In this chart, Kierkegaard's categories are paired with the analogous terms used by twentieth century theorists. The extreme left hand column indicates the range in duration of the types of despair being discussed, and the extreme right indicates the range in their corresponding objects. The issues of consciousness and volition are also important to outlining a taxonomy of despair, but because they are less straightforward, they are more difficult to plot in a schematic fashion. Let us turn, then, to a closer and more detailed examination of characteristic features of each of these types of despairing.

Despair as a "Negative, Contending Emotion"

Magda Arnold is a psychologist who has written extensively on human emotional life. Her works distinguish emotions from feelings and moods (a distinction we will flesh out in the next section of the taxonomy), using a classification scheme drawn from Aristotelian/Thomistic definitions. An emotion, she writes, is a "felt tendency toward or away from" an object which affects the experiencing subject; such a tendency can be of either the "impulse" (concupiscible) or "contending" (irascible) variety. Much like Thomas Aquinas, she posits that despair is that emotion which tends away from a desirable but inaccessible object in the face of obstacles to its possession which are judged to be insuperable. Hence, her designation: despair constitutes a "negative, contending emotion."[1] Aquinas' phrasing is slightly more euphonious: for him, this type of despair is an "irascible passion."

Consider a simple example of despair at this level. During the years that Isabel keeps house for her widowed and subsequently invalided father, she periodically despairs of the state of disarray into which it seems inexorably to be falling. "It was with despair that I went into the homes of my friends," she confesses, "homes cared for by mothers who knew what they were doing, who understood what had to be done with old magazines, with the smell at the bottom of the sink" (35). She, on the other hand, feels defeated by clutter and grime, by piles of old books and magazines "desiccating" on the floor, by rags and newspapers and flat-bristled scrub brushes threatening to overtake the broom closet. The condition of that closet, she

116

writes, "was a disorder that vanquished me in private and in public mortified me."

The type of despair which Isabel identifies here is clearly at the level which Magda Arnold's categorization describes. It is a "felt tendency" of aversion which turns away from a desirable object because there seem to be too many obstacles in the path toward its realization. Isabel would like a clean house, but she feels herself unable to muster the energy or the expertise necessary to achieve one. Consequently, she "turns away" from this specifically-desired object. She resigns herself to the belief that it is beyond her grasp. In a word, she despairs.

Because despair understood to be a "negative, contending emotion" is object-specific in this way, it also appears to be of relatively short or episodic duration. The despair over a cluttered broom closet does not occupy every moment of Isabel's waking consciousness. Rather, it recurs — regularly, but intermittently nonetheless — every time she has to open the door of that dreaded closet to retrieve something from its forbidding recesses. When she becomes engrossed in some other activity of the "balletic routine" of caring for her father, she is likely to forget the closet as well as the desiccating piles of old books and magazines on the floor, looking over them — overlooking them — in the course of focusing on more immediately pressing demands. Thus, despair as an object-specific emotion shows itself to be both fickle and fleeting: it is apt to disappear for want of receiving constantly devoted attention.

Even with this simple example, it is important to note that the "object" which elicits or "occasions" the despair does so within a framework of interpretation. That is to say, it is not the object in and of itself which induces despair, but rather the object-as-perceived: specifically, the object as perceived to be desirable and judged to be out of reach. I think it is fair to suppose that there are some people (though I am not among them) for whom a messy closet *never* induces despair, either because they do not consider tidiness a priority, or because they imperturbably proceed to tidy up when they need to rather than succumbing to paralysis at the prospect. This is significant inasmuch as it suggests that despair is always accompanied by "cognitive consorts," by attitudes and judgments whose presence is integral to the experience of the emotion itself. Thus, the question of healing despair must always attend not only to the occasioning/provoking situation (the "object"), but also to the complex of attitudes and perceptions (the framework of interpretation) within which that situation is assessed to be a "desperate" one.

The preceding remarks have direct implications for the question of corrigibility. Three points converge to indicate that the *object-specific emotion* (the first degree) of despair does stand amenable to a degree of control. The initial point concerns the fact of a clearly-defined object. Knowing specifically what the despair is about enhances the possibility of discovering resources for coping or overcoming. It is, after all, easier to prescribe and procure remedies for a precisely diagnosed malady than for a vague and unidentifiable assortment of ills. The second point concerns the fact of selective attention. If object-specific despair recedes when focus upon it is withdrawn, then diversions show some promise of helping (and Cassian's counsels of manual labor, or Luther's of merry-making, show their therapeutic wisdom once again). The third point concerns the possibility of modifying an interpretive framework. I can still hear the voice of my mother saying to me, "The only thing you can change about this situation is your attitude." For some forms of object-specific despair, such advice is assuredly (if soberingly) true. If the circumstances occasioning the despair cannot be altered, perhaps at least the cognitive consorts accompanying it can. Perhaps I can train myself (discipline myself to a mature "discernment," to hearken back to Evagrius) that some of the things which devastate me simply are not that important — at least not important enough to rob me of the spiritual vitality which is eaten away by despair.

To speak of attitude adjustment as a means of "correcting" despair does, however, presume that the experience of despair in question is not "irrational." Amélie Rorty offers a helpful definition: "a person's emotion," she writes, "is irrational if correcting the belief presupposed by the emotion fails to change it appropriately *or* if the person uncharacteristically resists considerations that would normally lead him [or her] to correct the belief."[2] Thus, Isabel's despair over the creeping clutter in her broom closet would be irrational were it to persist long after someone offered to help her with the cleaning — that is to say, long after her initial and despair-producing belief in the impossibility of the task had been exposed to friendly correction. The problem with the preceding analysis of corrigibility is that, by its very nature, despair seems to favor such irrationality. By its own particular phenomenological magnetism, it repels persuasion and dissuasion. We noted along with Kierkegaard a tendency for the person in despair to refuse even the most well-meaning assistance, to get caught up in playing endless rounds of Eric Berne's aptly named game of "Why Don't You; Yes But . . .": "If it bothers you so much, why don't you just clean out the closet?" "Yes, but I just don't know which of those old newspapers to throw away and which I ought to be saving." "Why don't you ask your father which he wants you to save?" "Yes, but he really isn't feeling well right now, so I hate to bother him with that kind of detail." "Why don't you let me help you with some of the sorting and cleaning?" "Yes, that's very kind of you, but I really don't want to take up your time with such a silly task." And so, on and on, it goes. In such circumstances, it seems almost as if despair seeks to perpetuate itself, characteristically (if "irrationally") attracting its own set of self-justifying excuses. Were it not for such irrational tendencies, the thwarting circumstances of our lives would issue in something more akin to frustration, rather than in the hope-denying, energy-killing excesses of despair.

All of which is by way of saying that the analysis of despair as an object-specific, negative contending emotion is not fully adequate to the nature of the experience. More often than not, despair has less to do with the particular object which is named as its provocation, and more to do with the general state of the subject who encounters it as provoking under a given set of circumstances. This "general state" may have a physiological component which, appropriately diagnosed, can enhance our understanding of the emotion. As Amélie Rorty observes: "When we look for the explanation of a recalcitrant inappropriate emotion, there is sometimes no need to look deeply into the etiology of the intention: the state of the person's endocrine system is explanation enough."[3] Some emotions, she continues, are primarily associated with physical states such as metabolic imbalance — an observation which casts an interesting modern scientific light on the ancient Greek theory of humoral psychology. The hypothesis of a "melancholic humor," which Hippocrates first posited and which Robert Burton revisited in the seventeenth century, now reappears in the twentieth century in theories which link despair with various mood disorders brought on by elevated levels of cortisol in the bloodstream or by malfunctions in norepinephrine or serotonin metabolism.[4] (Sometimes, it would seem, despair is clearly more a sickness than a sin.) Interestingly enough, however, such physiological conditions are referred to as "mood" rather than "emotional" disorders; we will turn to the distinction between a mood and an emotion momentarily as we move further through our taxonomy.

Sometimes, however, the physiological conditions alone do not appear as clearly relevant for explaining why a person is moved to despair in a particular situation. Sometimes the hormones are in balance and all else is functioning in prime condition, yet a sense of hopelessness still persists. At such times, in order to understand why a specifically-identified situation evokes a despair so irrationally intransigent that even an offer to change the situation does not bring relief, we need more information about what Rorty has just called "the etiology of the [emotion's] intention." In simple terms, we need to know where the despair is coming from, what it is *really* about. Although I may specify an object (like Isabel, I am in despair over the clutter and grime in my house), the chances are good that the real source of my emotion is something less specific and more entrenched (I am in despair because I have perfectionistic standards, for housework or work of other kinds, which I can never satisfactorily meet). So often, despair draws its sustenance from a wide-ranging complex of beliefs and attitudes which constitute the very substrate of my personal way of being in the world. Consequently, it is often of longer and more recurrent duration than its specified provocation would seem rationally to warrant. The external circumstances which I blame for my despair, the objects which I designate, are only a surface manifestation of a more profound phenomenon. Rooting deeply, despair can thus be exceedingly difficult to extirpate. Rooting deeply, despair thus ultimately (and radically) transcends the category of "negative, contending, object-specific emotion."

Despair as a "Generalized Emotion"

Kierkegaard has already recognized this transcendence in his continuum of analysis, wherein "despair over something earthly" so quickly spreads into "despair over the earthly *in toto*." Twentieth century phenomenologists of the passions have similarly noted such a movement, for which reason they have categorized despair differently from Magda Arnold — as something more akin to a *mood* than to an *emotion*. Robert Solomon proposes a median position between these designations. For him, despair is still an emotion insofar as it has an identifiable object. Yet, he says, in contrast to those emotions which almost always intend something specific (he cites the example of sadness), there are also emotions which typically intend something general. One example of such a "generalized emotion" is despair.[5]

Thus understood, despair is still not a mood. Moods, according to Solomon, are about "nothing in particular." When I am in a "good mood," (or a foul one, for that matter), I am hard-pressed to say exactly why. "Nothing in particular" has made me so chipper (or so irritable); I simply am. Even occurrences that might normally alter my affect leave it unchanged. I hit repeated snags in my work; "Ah well," I shrug, "It's no big deal." (I get repeated reinforcement from friends and colleagues; "So what," I grouse, "Big deal.") Whereas emotions arise in virtually predictable circumstances, targeting discriminate objects or provocations, moods come and go unpredictably, indiscriminately coloring all objects that lie within their path. Emotions are characteristically *about* something (I am angry at *him* for *this* reason). Moods are about everything and nothing simultaneously (I am anxious, and I don't know why).

Unlike moods, then, which are about "nothing in particular," despair — according to Solomon — is about "a particular generalized" (172). He describes the typical phenomenology of such "generalized emotions" in this way: "a particular incident seems to act as a catalyst, crystallizing out the ornate precipitate that soon becomes supersaturated consciousness" (172). In other words, one situation acts as the trigger for an emotion whose affective range then grows far more extensive than the single occurrence would seem to justify. Nettie leaves, and Celie is convinced that *no one* will ever find her lovable again; Isabel's father dies, and her consciousness grows "supersaturated" with the foreboding conviction that her life will never again have such a steady source of identity and fulfillment. In both these instances, despair refuses to confine itself to the particular, triggering losses. Rather, it sweepingly generalizes to reach foregone conclusions about *all* future possibilities for meaningful relationship.

Some of the terminology of the philosophical study of human emotions is useful for clarifying and articulating this point in another way. The terminology concerns the distinction between the "occasion" and the "object" of an affective experience. Succinctly put: the "occasion" is what prompts the emotion; the "object" is what it is over or about. Solomon's contention about the generalized nature of the object of despair has just insisted that occasion and object are not one and the same: the occasion is the "catalyst"; the object is the "supersaturated consciousness" which ensues. Returning to an example from Isabel's story in *Final Payments* makes this distinction even more explicit.

In Chapter Three, when illustrating Kierkegaard's description of the move from "despair over something earthly" to "despair over the earthly *in toto*," we looked briefly at an occurrence early in Isabel's efforts to reenter the world after the death of her father (and after the preceding eleven-year period during which she had confined herself to his care). As part of her initiation into a new job which she has landed, she must go to a function at the local Community Center to meet the staff of college-age students whom she will be supervising. She and they are getting along amicably, if a slight shade awkwardly, drinking beer and talking together. But then someone turns on the jukebox, and couples begin separating off to dance. The unfamiliar melodies and movements bring home to Isabel in a visceral fashion how out of touch she has become. Tears spring to her eyes and she rushes to the ladies' room to escape:

I closed the door of the booth and sat on the toilet, sobbing. No one must see me. What could I say? "I'm crying because I don't know any of the dances"? It was absurd. I sobbed into my cold hands (116).

The *occasion* of Isabel's sobs, "not knowing any of the dances," does indeed seem "absurd" and disproportionate to the pain which it engenders. But the *object* of her discomfort is far less localized and far less trivial. From the fleeting occasion of feeling out of touch, Isabel's despair, by its characteristic phenomenological dynamism, has "generalized" to encompass a lifetime of seemingly endless alienation and aloneness. The *occasion* of her despair is a moment; its *object*, however, is the assumption that such moments will submerge her entire out-stretching future.

The word "assumption" above is not casually chosen. It highlights the fact that the object of Isabel's despair is more aptly understood through an appraisal of attitudes and expectations in her mind than through a simple assessment of the occurrences in her surroundings. This is not to say that her despair is *all* "in her head." Far from it: the death of her father is real, as is the difficulty of forging a new way of being in the world after such a significant life-transition.[6] However, it *is* to say that her despair is an *active construal* of her situation, and not just a passive acquiescence to it. This insight, which we must now develop further, stands as a second valuable contribution of Robert Solomon's phenomenology of the "generalized emotion" of despair. (To anticipate where we are headed, this insight also has significant implications for the issue of "corrigibility," or the question of whether or not I can "help it" if I despair).

Solomon, in fact, defines emotions in terms of their dimension of attitudinal activity. Emotions, he says, are "*constitutive* judgments according to which our reality is given its shape and structure" (xix). Note how this definition helps to bridge the traditionally assumed split between affect and cognition, emotion and rationality. Emotions are ways in which we construe our worlds as meaningful and supportive or meaningless and self-defeating. Solomon cites despair as an example. In his analysis, despair consists of "a judgment of unhappy resignation, a conclusion of futility, an admission of defeat." In despair, a person "gives up hope and expectations, often never realizing that those hopes and expectations are themselves the products of judgments that might well be re-examined" (298).[7]

We have seen this to be the case with Isabel (and with a little honest introspection, we can see it to be the case with ourselves as well). Isabel "gives up hope and expectations" based on an "admission of defeat" which entails something far deeper than simply "not knowing the dances." Ultimately, her despair is over her own aloneness — and it is built on top of a set of assumptions that reads something like this: the one person who loved me and who made my life meaningful has died; in fact, any relationship which might ever confirm and fulfill me will be similarly subject to mortality, to separation and loss; therefore, the prospect of intimate relatedness is too fragile, too costly; aloneness, no matter how desperately painful, is to be preferred. But in Isabel's scene of "epiphany" which we have discussed in some detail in Chapter One, this set of assumptions is broken through with the realization/revelation of a profound paradox: life *is* brutal; yet life is also the locus of beauty and meaning. The joy of dancing while the bridegroom is present finally appears to Isabel to be worth the pain that will come when the dance must inevitably end. This new realization becomes the basis for her healing, the ground from which she is able to construct a set of "reexamined" judgments which enable her to look forward in hope rather than in "unhappy resignation" and despair.

Solomon's position on emotions — "generalized" or otherwise — as "constitutive judgments" has clear implications for the issues of corrigibility and accountability. To the question, "Can I help it if I despair?" his answer must follow as a resounding, "Yes." A central thesis of his work on *The Passions*, in fact, is that we have been duped by a "hydraulic model" of human emotion into thinking that we are at the mercy of various "blind or stupid forces" within us that *make* us feel certain ways, whether we like it or not. He argues just the contrary:

"I couldn't help it; I was angry"; "She's not responsible; she's in love"; "Don't blame him; he was embarrassed": These are symptoms of a malady that cuts far deeper than a merely faulty theory of human nature. These are the products of irresponsible self-deception, attempts to place blame and responsibility beyond ourselves for what, I shall argue, is in fact the most our own (148).

Solomon's argument is that not "blind forces" but *we ourselves* "make ourselves depressed, think ourselves into grief, contemplate our way to joy, and litigate our way into guilt" (418). The "blame" for our emotions lies no where beyond us, but rather in our own judging and world-construing capacities. This is a radical thesis. Solomon acknowledges, however, that he shares it (if a bit grudgingly) with certain "old moralists" of the Christian Church. "One of the few places in which we must side with traditional Christianity," he writes, "is on the matter of the voluntariness of the emotions" (191n). Perhaps, then, to speak of despair as a deliberate sin is not so very far afield after all (More on this in Chapter Five to come). At any rate, Solomon is adamant that an "ethics of emotion" requires that we "give up the self-excusing illusion that we *suffer* our emotions, . . . and [rather that we] see them as our own *creative activities*." If I am in despair, it is not that I *cannot* help myself, but rather that I *will not* do so (430–431, also 279).

The outgrowth of this ethical position of Solomon's is a bracing exhortation to "self-overcoming" (375). Once we recognize that our emotions are our ways of judging and construing our circumstances in self-affirming or self-defeating fashion, we can begin the discipline of maximizing our former "life-enhancing" tendencies and minimizing our "life-stultifying" ones (to use terminology from Nietzsche which Solomon finds compelling) (126). Despair is clearly a "life-stultifying" strategy: as we have seen in Isabel's and Celie's stories and as we doubtless know from our own experience, despair saps our vitality, depletes our coping resources, drains us of the will to move forward, to move outward, to be for or be with or simply be at all. "What is needed," Solomon writes, "is constant vigilance and a learned reflective ability to 'catch ourselves' in the midst of every small but significant act of self-degradation" (424). What is needed is something akin to Evagrius' study of the "demons" through attentive spiritual discernment.

Still, Solomon continues, "even this is not enough" (424). He realistically acknowledges: "The fact that we have constituted [our emotions] does not make them any less durable, nor does it guarantee that we shall have an easy time in trying to change them" (426). To see through our despair to the often-unexamined "judgment of unhappy resignation, conclusion of futility, or admission of defeat" which lies at its core does not in and of itself accomplish the transformation of such "life-stultifying" attitudes. Reflection and discernment must be supplemented by expression and action. We must "talk out" and "work out" our feelings, directly taking on the persons and circumstances that "initiated and fed" them. Solomon concludes, vigorously and positively: "To change our emotions . . . it is necessary to change our world, and perhaps *the* world as well" (424).

This is all well and good, and it serves (as I said earlier) as a bracing exhortation. And yet . . . Is it not precisely part of the defining dynamism of despair that we do *not* feel like "talking it out," that we — like Isabel and Celie — retreat into silence and shun companionship? Nor do we find in ourselves the energy to "work it out," to "change the world," to tackle the circumstances which seem to us so overwhelming and defeating. If we *did* have this energy, we would not be despairing in the first place. Solomon seems, thus, to have offered us something of a tautology: overcome your despair by not being in despair.[8] While his observations about the "generalizing" nature of the object of despair are enormously helpful and his analysis of the role of our judgments in actively construing our circumstances as despair-provoking is insightful indeed, his counsel of healing through "self-overcoming" seems a shade of unsatisfying. Admittedly, there are times when such counsel could prove highly effective. Assuredly, there are times when we could do more to think, talk, work, change, and "help ourselves" out of despairing conditions. But what of those times when the pain is so deep, so pervasive, and so paralyzing that no resources we can muster seem capable of mounting any resistance against it? Solomon would call this very question an example of the dangerous self-deception against which he has been cautioning us. I am more inclined, however, to call it a description of a level of human experience to which Solomon's analysis elects not to penetrate. To deal with this level thus requires that we move from Solomon to the next branch of our taxonomy.

Despair and Moods

Initially, we saw Solomon differentiate between an emotion and a mood on the basis of their object choice: an emotion is about something specific (or, in the case of despair, something generalized) while a mood is about "nothing in particular." Solomon goes on, however, to downplay this very distinction. The dividing line between emotions and moods, he modifies, is "not a sharp" one, and in fact "the relationship between emotion and mood is one of mutual support and even *identity*" (172, my emphasis). This eventual conflation of mood and emotion goes a long way toward explaining Solomon's ultimately sanguine conclusions about corrigibility. An emotion, as he defines it, is indeed capable of some "self-overcoming." Judgments can be reexamined and circumstances re-construed in an increasingly lucid and "life-enhancing" light. But what of moods — particularly if they do exemplify a distinctive breed of experience?

Moods, as Solomon first acknowledged, are more global and less discriminating than emotions in their scope. A mood spreads to encompass all objects in its path, whether they reasonably deserve the affective tone thrust upon them or not. When I am in a depressive mood, events that would customarily please me, or at least affect me indifferently, take on a jaundiced and unpleasant taint which it is exceedingly difficult to argue away. In fact, any such argument about the "unreasonableness" of my feelings and reactions will more likely intensify than dispel my dismal humor.

Irrationally inclusive in its objects, a mood is also erratic and unpredictable in its eliciting occasions. Fatigue can put me in a silly mood or a somber one; I can be elated for no clear reason at all. Moods seem to "come over" me and "catch" me unawares; the very phrases we use to talk about them imply a sense of passivity. Thus, moods can be singularly more "incorrigible" than their emotional counterparts. In his study of *Spirituality and Human Emotion*, Robert Roberts concludes, "Moods, like sensations, are not subject to rational adjudication."[9]

Roberts' position, thus, offers us an illuminating contrast to Solomon's. The two men are similar enough in their basic philosophy of the passions to make the differences between them all the more significant. Both agree that emotions are active responses to circumstances rather than passive sufferings of them. Solomon defines emotions as "constitutive judgments." Roberts defines them in a kindred fashion as "concern-based construals"; he writes, "An emotion is a way of 'seeing' things, when this 'seeing' is grounded in a concern" (95 and 15).

Because emotions are ways of seeing or construing our circumstances, it is possible rationally to assess and even to alter them. Here Roberts and Solomon further agree. Roberts suggests the following example:

> If I judge that the people in the car behind me are following me with some sinister intent, I may be right or I may be wrong, and the basis on which I judge may be rational or irrational. But that judgment may also be the basis of the construal that generates anger or fear or indignation, and if so, then the emotion itself is either right or wrong, either rational or irrational (95–96).

In other words, an emotion has a *reason* rooted in my attitudes and perceptions: I am frightened not simply because I see that there is a vehicle behind me, but because I esteem that vehicle to pose a threat. If I alter my perceptual attitude (if, for example, I recognize that the driver of the car behind me is simply signaling to me that he has spotted a speed trap ahead), I alter my emotion from one of fear to one of gratitude.

Moods, however — according to Roberts — do not function in this way. Moods do not have reasons, but *causes*. I am irritable *not* because three students are cutting my class, although I may try to palm my irritability off on this external factor. In fact, however, sometimes students cut and I shrug my shoulders in an indulgent fashion, or smirk in self-satisfaction that it is, after all, their loss. The specified objects of my general grouchiness, its ostensible "reasons," are not nearly as salient in providing an explanation for it as are its *causes*: I did not sleep well the night before; I succumbed to the temptations of white flour and sugar and caffeine at breakfast and my moody state is now registering the toll of a blood sugar plunge.

One way that occurs to me to make this distinction between a reason and a cause clearer for ourselves is to try a device of word-substitution. For example: when I say that I am irritable *because* the three students are cutting, I could equally sensibly say, without altering my meaning, that I am irritable *over the fact that* three students are cutting. But this substitution, which discloses a reason, will not work with a cause. I say (when I finally stop blaming my students and start taking responsibility for my own nutritionally disastrous breakfast) that I am irritable *because* I ate junk food. If I try to substitute words, however, and say that I am irritable *over the fact that* I ate junk, I have changed meanings from my original intent. *Reasons* are part of the grammar of emotions: emotions, as we have said before, are *over* something; they have objects which provide the (assessable, alterable) rationale for their existence. Moods, on the other hand, require a different terminology: they are not reliably or consistently over any particular thing; they do not have objects; rather, they are caused.

The "caused" nature of moods thus helps in explaining why Roberts claims they "are not subject to rational adjudication." It is neither rational nor irrational to be irritable after loading up on caffeine and refined sugar, just as it is neither rational nor irrational to feel an urge to scratch after being bitten by a mosquito. An assessment of rationality is simply inappropriate within the distinctive logic of moods. Similarly, it is not possible to alter a mood by understanding its causation in the same way in which it is possible to alter an emotion by understanding its rationale. I can change the way I construe my surrounding circumstances; I cannot manipulate my internal environment with the same degree of success. If a blood sugar imbalance is making me grouchy, about the best I can do is to attempt to control my *behavior* until such time as the mood eliciting the behavior dissipates. I can snarl inwardly but think twice and compel myself to smile outwardly, knowing that the inward urge to bite someone on the ankle will eventually wear away.

The preceding distinction between emotions and moods becomes directly relevant to the topic of despair when the mood under analysis is that of depression. Despair and depression are undeniably close kin. The "old moralists" of the Christian church acknowledged something of this kinship by the linkages they drew between *tristitia* and *desperatio* in their genealogies of vice. With the language and logic of emotions and moods now before us, we need to draw some more psychologically and philosophically discriminating linkages. With Solomon, I must concur that the dividing line between the two sorts of affect is not a sharp one; unlike Solomon, however — and like Roberts — I must insist that the relationship between the two cannot finally be conflated into one of "identity." In order to pursue these linkages most fruitfully, it will first be helpful to take a somewhat closer look at despair's kindred experience of depression.

The Mood of Depression

When discussing "object-specific" emotions earlier, I cited Amélie Rorty's observation to the effect that a "recalcitrant inappropriate emotion" may be most readily explained by a look at "the state of the person's endocrine system." Depression certainly provides a case in point. I may feel myself sinking into a blue funk and be at a loss to explain what in the world has "gotten into" me — until I look at my calendar and discover that nothing in the *world* need be held accountable, because the fluctuating levels of estrogen and progesterone in my own *body* are more than sufficient to account for my uncontrollable weepiness. Depression (like irritability from too much caffeine and white sugar) is "caused." I am depressed *because* of my menstrual hormonal imbalance; I am not depressed (at least, not in the same way) *over the fact that* my hormones are out of kilter.

In a far less transient and fluctuating fashion, I may be depressed because (not "over the fact that") I have one of a variety of physiologically-induced "mood disorders." The terminology is apt: The depression of unipolar or bipolar illness is in fact of the global, non-rational (neither rational nor irrational), non-alterable (at least not by simple reexamination of judgments or reconstrual of contexts) nature of a mood. Where a "normal" depression will work itself out in time, a "pathological" or "clinical" depression demands medical intervention. The difference between normalcy and pathology is best drawn in terms of symptoms and their duration. The *Diagnostic and Statistical Manual* of the American Psychiatric Association (the DSM-III, updated for publication in 1980), offers the following criteria to distinguish a "major affective disorder" from a normal and/or milder depressive condition.[10] First, "the mood disturbance must be prominent and relatively persistent." Second, "at least four of the following symptoms [must] have each been present nearly every day for a period of at least two weeks:

1. Poor appetite or significant weight loss (when not dieting) or increased appetite or significant weight gain
2. Insomnia or hypersomnia (sleeping excessively)
3. Psychomotor agitation or retardation (but not merely subjective feelings of restlessness or being slowed down)
4. Loss of interest or pleasure in usual activities, or decrease in sexual drive. . . .
5. Loss of energy; fatigue
6. Feelings of worthlessness, self-reproach or excessive or inappropriate guilt (either may be delusional)
7. Complaints or evidence of diminished ability to think or concentrate. . . .
8. Recurrent thoughts of death, suicidal ideation (thoughts), wishes to be dead or suicide attempts."

When such symptoms are present and persistent, the depressive mood in question originates at a depth where exhortations to "self-overcoming" will not suffice.[11] Before any such therapeutic counsel can be expected to take effect, the way must be prepared by medication to restore the sufferer to basic emotional health. As we heard (in Chapter Two) the scholastic David of Augsburg say: sometimes, when *acedia/tristitia* is brought on by an excess of the melancholy humor, "it behooves the physician rather than the priest [or moralist] to prescribe a remedy."

The physician's remedy alone, however, is not sufficient either (remember how Robert Burton classified melancholy as a "compound mixt malady" requiring multiple avenues of cure?). Even the medical experts acknowledge as much. Psychiatrist Demitri Papolos advises: "Simply relegating [depressive mood] disorders to the realm of physiological disturbances that require only medical treatment is a serious clinical oversight and a gross scientific presumption."[12] The additionally useful *cognitive therapy* which Papolos describes sounds, in fact, remarkably similar to some of Robert Solomon's recommendations.[13] Cognitive therapy, as developed by Dr. Aaron Beck, operates off the premise that a person's moods and emotions are shaped by his or her thoughts, such that a modification of the thought patterns can bring about a change in the affect which is experienced. Depressive thinking tends to focus selectively on negative features of the environment and on harsh assessments of the self. In particular, it magnifies external problems and internal deficiencies, drawing conclusions of hopelessness and helplessness in the face of the future. Cognitive therapy for depression, therefore, works to identify such distorting conclusions and to construct more affirmative approaches for confronting difficulties and shortcomings.

If this kind of cognitive therapy or "thought modification" will assist in overcoming even depressions of clinical magnitude, then how much more might it be effective in responding to the more normal despondent moods that occasionally infiltrate our lives? Such a question leads us back to the orienting issue of this chapter: can we, in fact, be fairly expected to "help ourselves" (think ourselves, talk ourselves, work ourselves) out of depression or despair? Just how directly "corrigible" are such experiences; just how "accountable" are we? Before coming to a concluding position on this issue, a few further words on the relationship between despair and depression need to be said.

Despair and Depression: Emotion and Mood

Now that we have explored the distinctive logic of various types of affective experiences and have looked more directly at the phenomenon of depression, we are in a position to suggest the overall formula: despair relates to depression as an emotion (albeit a "generalizing" one: here we ultimately agree with Solomon) to its most characteristically accompanying mood. Depression is clearly the broader, more encompassing experience: it is characterized by numerous features (lassitude, excessive sleeping, feelings of worthlessness and anxiety, restlessness and inability to concentrate), a *particular one* of which is hopeless ideation — in other words, despair. Once again, we see the "old moralists" of the Christian church to have been perceptive in their diagnosis: *tristitia/acedia*, the parent sins, possess a number of progeny — *otiositas, somnolentia, inquietudo, instabilitas mentis et corporis* — in addition to desperatio. Despair, then, marks itself off from the more encompassing "parent" category — most specifically by demanding an element of awareness and a specific type of thinking.

To clarify this assertion, it is useful to consider the question: Can I be in despair without being aware of my condition? For Kierkegaard, as we saw in Chapter Three, the answer would have been a qualified, "yes." That is to say, as he understands it, existing in despair does not necessitate the recognition that one is despairing. In fact, the initial, "unpotentiated" variants of the "sickness unto death" consist in large measure of ignorance of the malady. Even the more self-conscious forms of the sickness — those of "weak," nonwilling despair or of despair which is "defiant" and willful — express themselves in exactly opposite ways, further confusing the possibility for self-diagnosis. Kierkegaard is so keenly aware of our human opacity to our foibles and failings that he is loath to allow introspection as a valid means whereby we may come to recognize our own psychological or spiritual state. What I *think* I feel, for Kierkegaard, frequently offers the most misleading cues as to how I actually am. This is especially true in the instance of despair, whose very *duplicity* (recall that the Danish *Fortvivlelse* is constructed around the etymological root meaning "two") serves to distort the perception of its own cause and cure. Therefore, it is quite common — indeed, in Kierkegaard's judgment, virtually universal — for persons to be in despair, in a state of doubleness, brokenness, and alienation, without recognizing or acknowledging our condition to be as such.

It is telling, however, that the preceding summary of Kierkegaard's position equates being in despair with existing in a *state* of brokenness. For, in fact, Kierkegaard does finally conceive of despair more as a *structure* of existence than as a phenomenon of experience. The problem with this idiosyncratic usage is that it so expands the notion of despair as to rob the term of its specificity as an emotion concept. As a result, the approach to healing despair suffers significant impoverishment, as we saw toward the close of Chapter Three. Kierkegaard by-passes the specificity of psychological measures of healing because he is ultimately looking for salvation from the unseen structures of sinfulness rather than for solace from the felt pains of despairing. While the latter, phenomenological pains may provide a close psychological analogue for the former, theological condition, the two cannot be completely equated. Sin is more than the absence or abandonment of hope (even of the hope for salvation); despair is less than the total alienation of persons from the source and sustenance of their being (though it may provide a particularly potent symptom thereof). Thus, to say that, because of structural brokenness, we all exist "in despair" — even though we are not consciously aware of its presence — seems to stretch the boundaries of the concept beyond the limits of linguistic accuracy (at least in English usage) or experiential validity.

To put this in another way, let us attempt to contrast two statements: "Isabel is depressed, but she does not know it"; and "Isabel is in despair, but she does not know it." The former statement makes some sense. We may notice that Isabel is dragging through the "balletic routine" of caring for her invalid father. She may still be functioning efficiently, but it is more in the sense of a mechanistic going-through-the-motions than anything else. She spends more and more time sleeping. She rarely speaks to anyone or leaves the house. If one were to ask how she was feeling, doubtless she would put on a brave front and respond that everything was, "Fine, just fine." But behavioral observations over a period of time can lead us to a reasonably accurate diagnosis that she is depressed, although she has not yet allowed herself to acknowledge the depression at a conscious level.

The second sentence, however, does not seem to function in quite the same way — unless we are simply conflating the meanings of the words despair and depression (and thereby, I would suggest, diminishing both our linguistic and our affective repertoires). While it can make sense to diagnose Isabel as being depressed without her being conscious of it, to say that she is in despair "unawares" appears more problematic. The precise meaning of despair expresses that sense of futility or defeat that accompanies a loss of hope. However, hope — like despair — demands the presence of *expectations* and the *appraisal* of whether or not these bear any promise of fruition. Both functions, expecting and appraising, require a cognitive dimension. Therefore, we may say that, by its very definition, despair entails awareness: Isabel is in despair over the state of her broom closet because she is thinking about its insidious clutter and about the seeming impossibility of finding the time, energy, or know-how to weed through it; she is in despair over "not knowing any of the dances" because she is attending to her feelings of alienation and her fears for a perennially lonely and barren future. Despair demands awareness and a particular kind of thinking — a thinking which looks upon the self as resource-less and upon the future as thwarting of heart-felt desires.

Despair, then, is more like an emotion than a mood. It does not occupy our experience simply "because" (because of hormonal imbalance or lack of sleep, for example). Even if such factors are present and contributing, when we identify our experience as *despair* we do so insofar as it is also "over the fact that" (over the fact that we have looked to the future and to ourselves and have found both sorely wanting). While depression can be preeminently "caused," despair is distinctively "reasoned." We must grant, however, that its "reasons" may seem irrational to someone who is not aware of their rooting in the very depths of our self-and world-appraisals. We must also grant that despair's most characteristic "objects" are expansive ones — ones which engulf increasingly large proportions of our life-world, until our despair over a particular provocation becomes despair over the whole human condition, at which point the global nature of the experience closely resembles the phenomenology of a mood.

In fact, the generalizing tendency of the emotion of despair seems to predispose it to spread and overspill until it ends in the mood of depression. Robert Roberts points to this as one of the characteristic linkages between an emotion and its affiliate mood. As he notes, "grief at the death of a loved one can 'color' one's entire outlook on life for a period; the grief, which is clearly an emotion, begets a generalized depression, which is not an emotion but a mood" (97). The same appears true of despair. The loss of hope for a cherished project or plan can twist and distort our whole field of vision, spiraling us downward into depression. Once we become depressed, however, it is no longer simply our hopes, but rather our whole being which is affected. At this point, what the "old moralists" called the "sister" — the affiliate or companion — characteristics of despair appear: the restlessness, the feelings of self-reproach, the anxiety, the overall paralysis of the will.

Nor does the linkage between despair and depression run only one way. Roberts continues his analysis of the interrelationships in the following fashion:

> . . . the fact that moods are sometimes caused by emotions is not the only connection between the two. Moods also *predispose* emotions. I am, for example, more likely to dwell on the happy aspects of my future (and thus to experience hope) if I am in an even, optimistic, cheerful mood than if I am depressed (97).

By the same token, I am more likely to appraise my future as thwarting and forbidding if I am feeling otherwise "low." In other words, just as the emotion of despair can expand into a globally depressive mood, so the mood of depression can focus itself into a nodal point of despair. Thus, in order to "help myself" out of despairing I will ultimately need to address not only the set of expectations and appraisals which colors my future as barren and myself as unable or unworthy to effect change within it; I will also need to address the mood of depression which predisposes me to arrive at and dwell upon such disheartening assessments.

Concluding Question: Can I "Help" my Despairing?

We began this chapter with the outline of a taxonomy of types or levels of despairing: despair as an object-specific, "negative contending" emotion (analogous to Kierkegaard's "despair over something earthly"); despair as a "generalizing emotion" (paralleling Kierkegaard's "despair over the earthly *in toto*"); and despair as a mood (akin to Kierkegaard's assessment of despair as a deep-seated alienation of the total self). Now that we have examined each of these varieties of experience in turn, we are in a position to suggest a slightly different taxonomy — one which offers greater linguistic precision for the phenomenon of despairing, marking it off from its kindred affective experiences, all the while noting the integral interconnections among them.

The modified taxonomy suggests the following schematic:

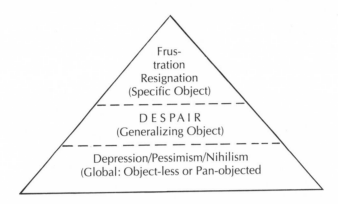

Frus-
tration
Resignation
(Specific Object)

– – – – – – – – – –

D E S PA I R
(Generalizing Object)

– – – – – – – – – – – –

Depression/Pessimism/Nihilism
(Global: Object-less or Pan-objected

What the pyramid above denotes is a tier of related affective experiences, differentiated according to the range of their characteristically targeted objects. For example: at the narrowest, perhaps even the most superficial point of the affective repertoire, the emotional response to the thwarting of a specific desire (or, in the terminology of Aristotle, Aquinas, and Magda Arnold, the felt tendency of aversion from an object which is desired but deemed inaccessible) is most accurately termed "frustration" or "resignation." The choice between these two terms depends upon the degree to which some desire for the object remains lively: in frustration, I continue to yearn and hope, however aware I may be of the futility of such actions; in resignation, I abandon hope altogether.

At the deepest and broadest base of the pyramid, in contrast, my affect is so expansive as to target no particular object but rather to infiltrate every object within my life-world. The clearest designation for this kind of experience, as we have seen, is that of "depression." The *mood*-like quality of depression finds parallels and supports in a certain *modality* of attitudes: in a tacit "philosophy of life" which orients me toward pessimistic or nihilistic assessments of self, world, and others; in a disposition to focus on the problems rather than the potentials of any given situation; in what Richard R. Niebuhr would call an "attunement" — a habitual and pervasive tonality of my very way of making sense out of my experience.[14]

In between these two extremes — between the specificity of frustration/resignation and the universality of depression/pessimism — lies the middle range properly assigned to despair. Unlike the range of the mood/modality below it, despair does have its discriminate objects. Unlike the emotion above it, however, these objects are so deeply embedded in my scale of values that their thwarting tends to threaten my very ability to affirm that life in general, and my life in particular, is worth the pain of living. A less important object would not affect me so profoundly. At bottom, then, every occasion of despair culminates in the personally important, "generalized" object of my *self* in its *global* orientation toward the outstretched future and the surrounding world.

The point of this taxonomy is not simply to differentiate despair from its affiliated affective states. It is also to insist upon the permeable boundaries among these various levels. Thus, despair cannot be healed in isolation from efforts to rectify frustrating circumstances, on the one hand, or from endeavors to treat depression or to temper philosophical pessimism, on the other. To work simply at the first two levels, if they are symptomatic of an undergirding mood or modality, would be like pulling up the top of a weed but leaving its root system intact. To work simply at the level of the mood — particularly in terms of its physiological causation — would be like amputating a limb without going on to offer the necessary rehabilitative therapy.

The two taxonomies of this chapter, therefore, provide a needed framework for responding to the question, "Can I help my despairing?" As I reflect systematically on my circumstances, I recognize that I *can* help myself in differing ways at differing levels of the taxonomy, at the same time as I come to the sobering (or is it salutary?) realization that at some levels, I cannot help myself at all. I can modify some of the frustrating circumstances of my life; I can solicit outside help (including wide-ranging political action) in modifying some others. I can attend to some of the physiological factors that are operative in the causation of depressive moods: I can watch my diet, get proper sleep and exercise, seek medical care should severe depressive symptoms arise. I can work at the level of "attitude adjustment," attenuating a philosophical pessimism with a less "life-stultifying" world view, or adapting the "cognitive consorts" of my experience such that I do not generalize from helplessness and hopelessness in a particular situation to helplessness and hopelessness in myself and in the world at large.

However, it is at this point that the contrast between Robert Solomon and Robert Roberts becomes instructive once again. Earlier in our taxonomy, we heard Solomon exhort us to self-overcoming, out of his conviction that emotions (including moods) are constitutive judgments which are amenable to rational revision. While agreeing with Solomon in certain premises, Roberts is ultimately less sanguine than he about our chances for successful "self-help" at all levels.

Like Solomon, Roberts defines emotions as constructs — not strictly as "judgments," but nonetheless as "concern-based construals." Unlike Solomon, however, he concludes from this definition:

> The fact that emotions are construals goes a long way toward explaining how we have control over them, and also why we sometimes fail to control them when we try (21).

Because emotions are construals, we can induce them more or less voluntarily by "coming to see [our] situation in certain terms" (22). This is clearly verifiable: we all know how we can work ourselves up into a fuming fury by focusing upon the wrongs — real or imagined — which we have been made to suffer. By the same token, we can dispel an emotion by learning to view our circumstances in a different light. But this is the tricky part — because, as Roberts acknowledges, "'seeing' is a little bit like imagining," and imagination cannot always be bidden at will. Sometimes I can imagine "on demand," as when I pause in my writing or teaching in order to "think up" an illustration for a particular point. But sometimes, no matter how relentlessly I probe, no image will "come to mind" (the phrase itself implies some of the autonomy of imaginal life). And sometimes, on especially felicitous days, images bound into consciousness unsolicited — even as moods, like blissfulness or depression, overtake me with blatant disregard for any efforts on my part to conjure or control them. Or, as Roberts concludes, in line with the central concerns of this chapter:

> . . . it is the same with emotions. Sometimes I am hopeful without trying, sometimes I can make myself hopeful by trying to see promise in my situation, and sometimes I cannot make myself hopeful no matter how hard I try (22).

Thus, not only is it true of *moods* that they are, as we cited earlier, "not subject to rational adjudication." It is also true of *emotions* that, because of their link with our occasionally intractable imagination, that they are not always amenable to rational dissuasion or volitional "self-overcoming."

What is true of emotions in general seems to be particularly true in the instance of despair. While it is the case that I can cultivate my imaginative faculties through their education and exercise, and that I can discipline my affective faculties by learning to attend more closely to certain features of my context and less closely to others — in short, while it is the case, even for Roberts, that "our emotions are intractable less often than we would like to [think]" (23) — nevertheless, a crucial part of the symptomatology of despair is precisely the depletion of those imaginative energies which are necessary for the tasks of disciplined attention and creative re-construal. As we saw in Chapter One with Isabel's and Celie's experiences, despair is so devastating precisely because it saps the vitality of the spirit. The times when we need our energies of creative resistance the most are the times when we feel least capable of marshaling any energy at all. We would rather just sleep or eat furtively in our room; life itself seems "an awful strain."

William Lynch, whose book *Images of Hope* we will visit more fully in our culminating chapter, offers an insight in this regard which is akin both to Roberts' conceptual framework and to Isabel's and Celie's experiences. In Lynch's analysis, despair "lies exactly in the constriction of the private imagination." "What happens in despair," he concludes, "is that the private imagination . . . reaches the point of the end of inward resource and must put on the imagination of another if it is to find a way out."[15] With Roberts, Lynch observes that the imagination is that faculty which preeminently construes our circumstances as open or closed, as promising or forbidding. With Roberts, he also acknowledges that this imagination is not always subject to our personal command. With Mary Gordon and Alice Walker, authors of the exemplary stories of Isabel and Celie, Lynch comes to the vital conclusion that communion is necessary for the conquest of despair — because the "communal imagination" is able to discern and to offer gifts of healing possibility which the "constricted imagination" of the despairing individual may simply be unable to see.

Can I, then, "help" my despairing? An honest answer must entail both a yes and a no. There are many things which I *can* do to help myself — we have reviewed a number of these in the paragraphs above. Yet there also comes a point where I reach the end of my individual resources, where I can no longer imagine a leaven of possibility in a world which feels so oppressively "flat" to me. At this point, an in-breaking from outside my immediate limitations becomes necessary: an "epiphany"of unexpected insight; an offering of much-needed encouragement, empowerment, and assistance from my surrounding communities.

Thus, it would finally be unfair to place total responsibility for despair and its healing on my — or on any sufferer's — individual shoulders. Matters of communal accountability are also involved — matters of the community's complicity in creating the circumstances which frustrate any of us to the point of despairing; matters of the community's social responsibility to help us in remedying such circumstances; matters of the community's deep calling to participate with us in discovering those resources and possibilities which will break through the "constrictedness" of our private imaginations.

In the final analysis, then, to speak of such communal accountability is to open new dimensions in the traditional understanding of despair as sin. On the one hand, it is to suggest that such a designation has at least as much to do with the general brokenness of the situation out of which despair arises as it has to do with the personal deficiencies of the individual who is despairing. On the other hand, it is to underscore that the healing of despair often comes at least as much from resources outside the individual as it comes from resources within. To speak of these new dimensions of understanding draws us back into the vocabulary of the "old moralists" of the Christian Church — a vocabulary which makes ready use of terms like "fallenness" and "grace." Such old, conventional terms call for fresh elaboration within a contemporary theological understanding of the sin/sickness of despair. It is to this task that we now turn in our culminating chapter.

CHAPTER 5

Theological Reflections:
Dialectics and Dance

We closed the last chapter with a contrast between two ways of answering the question whether or not we can "help" our despairing. One answer was that of Robert Solomon, who maintains a staunch affirmative: yes, we *can* help ourselves; we can reconstruct our despair-inducing judgments of defeat and futility through the rigorous practice of "self-overcoming." The contrasting answer was that of Robert Roberts (and, briefly introduced, that of William Lynch as well). Yes and no, they qualify. Many times we can help ourselves through precisely the kind of discerning self-discipline which Solomon recommends. Yet sometimes, even our bravest efforts to pull ourselves out of despondency will be to no avail.

Roberts and Lynch indicate three possible lines of explanation for such failure. First, our emotions — like despair — both grow out of and spill over into the kindred affective state of *moods*. Yet moods — "inaccessible to rational adjudication," "caused" rather than "reasoned," influenced by such internal factors as the state of our blood sugar level or our endocrine glands — can be exceedingly difficult to manipulate and dispel. Second, emotions — like despair — are "imaginative construals" of the circumstances in our life-world. Yet our imaginative powers have their own spontaneity and "intractability"; we cannot always command them to our will. Third, the emotion of despair in particular indicates to us the limits of the "private imagination." We fall into despair precisely because we as individuals can see no way out of our present predicament; our resources and our powers of creative resistance seem to us to have come to an end. We *despair* inasmuch as we feel the burden of being overwhelmingly impotent to "help ourselves." This does not mean, however, that we cannot be helped at all. It does, however, shift the onus from us as isolated and "private" individuals charged with the heroic task of "self-overcoming," to us as communities of individuals who are charged with the calling to bear burdens for and with one another.

These two ways of responding to the question of "self-helping" suggest a parallel — albeit an imperfect one — between the perspectives on despair which emerge out of Roman Catholicism and Protestantism, respectively. Robert Solomon, in fact, professes his (reluctant) alignment with "traditional Christianity" on the matter of the voluntariness of emotions. The tradition he means is clearly that of the "old moralists" like Evagrius and Cassian who considered despair as an offshoot of *acedia/tristitia* to be sinful, and who consequently exhorted their readers to the practice of remedial virtues such as patient discernment and vigorous courage. Robert Roberts, on the other hand, skeptical of the potential successes of human struggles for self-mastery, seems more clearly to draw from a Lutheran/Kierkegaardian heritage. While he, too, would have us work to cultivate virtues in ourselves — particularly the virtue of hope which serves to counter despair — he nonetheless acknowledges that our solitary powers of imagination and will are not always sufficient for the task of such cultivation. Finite and fallible as we surely are, we stand in further need of empowering grace.

The responses of Solomon, Roberts, and Lynch to the question of whether or not we can "help" our despairing begin thus to draw us back into the currents of Christian theological reflection. But before re-immersing ourselves in those currents, we would do well to pause and formulate the issues which will help us steer our course through this concluding chapter of theological exploration. The first issue is that just raised — the matter of characteristic Roman Catholic and Protestant approaches to despair and its healing. This issue brings into sharpest focus a dialectic of effort and grace which appears to be operative in any theological understanding of how despair can be overcome. Our second guiding issue moves from the sectarian designations of Catholic and Protestant to the broader designation of Christianity itself, seeking to uncover what it is that the Christian confession has helpfully and distinctively to say to the person who is despairing. This confessional answer centers on three key moments of the Christian story: the crucifixion, the incarnation, and the promise of eschatological *shalom*. Our third guiding issue then becomes that of discerning how the traditional Christian story shapes itself to address the particular needs of the present day. This shaping highlights three essential emphases for a contemporary constructive theology of human despairing: an emphasis on confessionalism (rather than Christocentric exclusivism); an emphasis on courage (rather than on humility); and an emphasis on communal responsibility (rather than on individual redemption from sin).

Catholic and Protestant Approaches: The Dialectic of Effort and Grace

The Catholic Approach

The Roman Catholic strand in the history of ideas of despair — the strand of the "old moralists" from the patristic to the scholastic periods — expresses a clear emphasis on what Robert Solomon has called the "voluntariness of the emotions." In this tradition, sin is primarily considered an *act* of wrongly-directed will, an act eluding the control of "right reason," an act inimical to a life of disciplined and cultivated virtue. Despair becomes a sin when it deliberately turns way from the theological object of the *bonum divinum*, the divine good, perversely and irrationally rejecting God's promises of forgiveness and benediction. Despair becomes a sin when it saps our vitality to the point where we can no longer marshal any resources for the practice of charity. If we despair, ultimately it is we ourselves who bear the responsibility. Rather than look to the discouragements and frustrations of our immediate futures, we should work to focus upon God's ultimate future of resolution and reconciliation as the source of tempering and transcendent hope. Our will stands in control.

There is much wisdom in the approach of this tradition. The "old moralists" of the Christian church harbor few illusions about human tendencies to self-pitying self-indulgence. Theirs is a rigorous morality which stresses the conquest of demons and the cultivation of vigorous and hearty virtues. Even the sternness of their injunction, "You are forbidden to despair!" conceals in itself a pastoral intent. For underneath this commandment sounds the message of reassurance: "Whoever you are, whatever you have done, whatever has happened to you, you are forbidden to believe that you have passed outside the reach of God's sustaining love." By calling despair a "sin," the old moralists emphasize the gravity of the temptation to give up on oneself as a child of God. Such a temptation must be rooted out by forceful measures. Patience, fortitude, hope, and joy: these are the remedial virtues to be *practiced* and *perfected*. Self-discipline and spiritual effort will eventually bear fruit in a triumph over despair.

Yet even this vigorous tradition does not treat the theme of effort and "self-overcoming" without an awareness of the complexities of the question of volition. Karl Rahner and Waldemar Molinski, both contemporary Catholic theologians, carry forward the heritage of patristic and scholastic thinking on this question in significant ways. In the following passage, Rahner urges an important — and typically Thomistic — distinction:

> In theology, despair is the sin of *freely* abandoning hope, which relies on God's faithfulness, help, and mercy in all our jeopardy and distress, without or within. . . . *Passive experience* of one's jeopardy and impotence is *not*, as such, despair in the theological sense.[1]

Like Aquinas, Rahner here emphasizes the criterion of willfulness as one which differentiates despair as a sin from despair as a mere amoral passion of the "irascible appetite."

Molinski, writing in the Catholic compendium edited by Rahner, the *Sacramentum Mundi*, carries this distinction even

146

further. From his perspective, despair as a sin entails a *"voluntary* rejection of a *consciously recognized* dependence of man [*sic*] upon his fellowmen and upon God."[2] Consequently, before people in despair can be assessed as sinning, they must be known to recognize their "duty to place hope in God and neighbor" and to be capable of "the personal relationships which enable them to perceive and accept the love of another." Some people, though, appear unaware of this "duty" and/or incapable of this act of acceptance. For a variety of tragic reasons, situations exist "when proffered love cannot be recognized as such," or when persons do not "possess sufficient will-power to respond to it and to open [themselves] trustingly to others and to God." One reason a person may fail to recognize or respond to love can be located in *pathology* — in one of the "many forms of melancholy . . . which induce feelings of despair and block either partially or completely the capacity to form relationships." Considered in these terms, the despair engendered by clinical depression is clearly more *sickness* than sin. Molinski here brings into contemporary idiom the insights of scholastic theologians such as John of Wales, Guillaume d'Auvergne, Alexander of Hales, and David of Augsburg, who wrote of the variant of despair brought on by an "abundance of the melancholic humors": "It behooves the physician rather than the priest to prescribe a remedy."[3]

Beyond pathology, a second set of reasons can also interfere with a person's ability to respond to "proffered love" or to "place hope in God and neighbor." These reasons root in *social conditions*. Molinski observes that there is a type of despair which "results from a [person's] inability to see God and other [people] as anything but enemies who wish him [or her] evil." If individuals are "unworthily treated," deprived of the opportunity of "experiencing the joy of another's love," or harassed by "the incomprehensible and bitter experiences" of personal fate, they may be "driven" to such desperation. Celie's story of physical and psychological brutalization comes immediately to mind as a case in point. Under circumstances such as hers, the *sin* is not so much her personal despair, but rather the system of racism, sexism, and economic injustice which drives her to it.

Thus, even in the Roman Catholic analysis, something more than a failure of individual effort can be involved in launching a person into despair, and something more than the successes of individual volition must be involved in setting a person free. As a result of such reasoning, however, the question of sin and volition begins to change terms. Rather than the product of a deliberate, individual sinful *act*, despair in certain instances comes to be seen as the outgrowth of a wider and corporate *state* of sinfulness. It is to this change in terms that the Protestant analysis of despair and volition in the writings of Luther and Kierkegaard primarily attends.

The Protestant Perspective

Where the Catholic tradition of patristic and scholastic as well as contemporary thinkers has focused on defining "when" despair becomes sinful due to its object, its irrationality, or its degree of volition, the Protestant line of thinking since Luther has eschewed such distinctions in favor of an overarching focus on defining "why." Why is despairing sinful? Simply put, because it reflects the fundamental and tragic breach between creature and Creator. From this Protestant perspective, *any* object of despair — and even the objectless despair which shades into the mood of depression — serves to illustrate the brokenness of a sinful and fallen world. The very fact that I abandon hope because of some disappointment regarding a "lesser" concern indicates a misdirection of my desires and a failure in following the imperative to "Rejoice in the Lord *always!*" Such a failure cannot be assessed or excused by looking to the question of volition or non-volition. Should I be overwhelmed by hopelessness due to temporary or temperamental weakness rather than due to deliberate rejection of a more hopeful and joyous alternative, *that very weakness* signals the distortion and enervation of a fallen will. Thus, despair for both Luther and Kierkegaard becomes the very paradigm for the state of sinfulness. Why? Because it exacerbates the estrangement between me and the sources of my being and well-being, and it impedes my trustful and celebrative affirmation of God's good creation.

However, it is not simply my personal brokenness which is at issue in the Lutheran/Kierkegaardian analysis of sin as the failure of faith. Rather, the whole human community has strayed from its original and intended harmony. As a sad consequence of this estrangement, occasions which provoke despairing tragically abound. "Principalities and powers" are afoot in the guise of persons, structures, and situations which destructively undermine the forces of hopefulness. Such destruction from without becomes all the more possible and pernicious because the individual as well has sinned and fallen away from the sources which should sustain a sense of ultimate assurance even in the face of proximate impossibility. Despair thus offers experiential testimony to the existence and interconnectedness of personal and corporate sin.

It is important to underscore that a distinctive definition of sin is operative here, however — a definition which runs counter to our accustomed assumptions that a sin is an act of moral wrongdoing, like gambling or gossiping or engaging in sexual indiscretions. Where Karl Rahner and Waldemar Molinski provided contemporary voices for the Roman Catholic emphasis on sin as a deliberate act contrary to virtue, Paul Tillich provides a twentieth-century voice for the divergent Lutheran/Kierkegaardian understanding. In his famous "You Are Accepted" sermon, Tillich rhetorically inquires:

> Have the [people] of our times still a feeling of the meaning of sin? Do they, and do we, still realize that sin does *not* mean an immoral act, that "sin" should never be used in the plural, and that not our sins, but rather our *sin* is the great, all-pervading problem of our life? . . . To be in the state of sin is to be in the state of separation.[4]

It is this *state* of separation, this *singularity* of sinfulness which despair dramatically illustrates. Thus, when theologians from the Protestant tradition describe despair as sinful, they are not so much denouncing the individual deficiencies of the person who is suffering; rather, they are decrying the universal tragedy of which we are *all* simultaneously accomplice and victim.

To speak of universal victimization by forces provocative of despair is to open a new dimension in the discussion of healing. If we have all tragically fallen away from the sources of both individual and communal *shalom*, then we all stand in need of a kind of reconciliation and whole-making which we, in our brokenness, cannot be expected to supply. Thus, counterbalancing the Catholic emphasis on *effort*, on the cultivation of rigorous virtues, stands the Protestant emphasis on *grace*, on the inbreaking of salutary strength from beyond.

Paul Tillich, again, enunciates this perspective. Despair, he writes:

> is an ultimate or "boundary-line" situation. One cannot go beyond it. Its nature is indicated in the etymology of the word despair: without hope. No way out into the future appears. Nonbeing is felt as absolutely victorious.[5]

Yet, he continues, "there is a limit to its victory; nonbeing is *felt* as victorious, and feeling presupposes being" (55). Even this modicum of "being," of the power which is necessary for despair to make itself felt, attests to an undergirding affirmative energy which can be the source of gracefully restorative courage. "Even in the state of despair," Tillich insists, "one has enough being to make despair possible" (177). To sense the presence of this "being" is to sense the presence of a persistent power which enables us to continue saying "Yes", even in the face of the most radical threats to our self-affirmation (180).

The Tillichian language may be abstract, but the point is palpable and profound. Even at the deepest pitch of despair, when "no way out into the future appears," when we cannot foresee any end to our current suffering or any hope for a happy resolution, there come moments — unpredictable, uncontrollable, fortuitous — when we find ourselves renewed by the power and capacity to move forward. Isabel experiences this dramatically in the scene of her epiphany. Out of the depths of the apathy into which she has retreated, closing herself off from the "extravagant affections" which she fears will expose her to loss and grieving, she senses a sudden and unanticipated upsurge of conviction: "I knew now," she affirms, that "I must open my life" (244). After so many days and weeks of closure, after the descent from specific despairing into an all-pervasive depression, after the deliberate deadening of any resources of her "private imagination," from where does this newly-energizing conviction originate? Isabel experiences it as a gift, a grace. Tillich, in his own distinctive language, agrees. We are "not necessarily aware of this source," he writes. "But it works in [us] as long as [we maintain] the courage to take [our] anxiety upon [ourselves]" (191). Unable though we may be to identify its origins, the experiential reality is that healing energy does come washing into the parched places of our lives — often when we least expect it, often when we are most in need.

This Tillichian answer is both satisfying and unsatisfactory at the same time. It is satisfying inasmuch as it identifies a type of mysterious and gracious healing to which many of our own experiences, like Isabel's, can attest. It is unsatisfactory inasmuch as it leaves us with the theological and profoundly personal question of why such grace suddenly becomes available at some moments yet remains intractably absent at others. The Psalmist's frequent lament, "How long, O Lord?" repeatedly sounds through our own voices. It is not a question to which Tillich (or Kierkegaard, or Luther) attempts an answer. Amazing grace remains precisely that: amazing — mystifying and defying all our attempts to conjure or control it. Healing *does* happen; the "power of being" does come breaking through, whether in a flash of epiphany or in the unexpected activity of a community of friends and advocates who take it upon themselves to address our need. Genuine though it be, such inbreaking — whether spiritual or social — eludes both our mastery and our desires for predictability. When we find ourselves emerging out of despair as the result of such experiences, our emergence *feels* more like a gift than a product of our personal efforts of will.

This phenomenological emphasis — on the felt experience of recovery — characterizes Tillich as well as his predecessors in the Protestant tradition. Luther, too, has named it: "Just when I was in death's deepest throes and had the least hope," he acknowledges, in speaking about one of his bouts with *Anfechtung*, "the Lord came . . . and by a miracle led my life out of death and destruction."[6] Yet, just as the Roman Catholic strand of Christian tradition does not speak of effort apart from a sensitivity to the complexities of the question of volition, and even the most ascetic of "old moralists" would not pretend that the cultivation of virtues can be done apart from God's grace, so in the Protestant strand of tradition, the emphasis on grace

151

is counterbalanced by some awareness of the need for human exertion. Less so in Kierkegaard, who pays little attention to measures short of divine atonement by which human beings may receive solace from the sickness unto death, as we have seen. Perhaps also, less so in Tillich, who has been accused of a certain quietism in his descriptions of how we experience the inbreaking of "the courage to be."[7] But their mutual predecessor Martin Luther is keenly attuned to the dialectic of human activity in consort with divine gifts of healing — or, better, is attuned to the multiple mediations through which the grace of God may choose to become manifest. Thus, Luther counsels us variously to tear out the darts of the devil by force; to seek out the companionship of others; to get downright angry; to "be merry . . . both inwardly in Christ and outwardly in his gifts and the good things of life."[8] Effort and grace, exertion and *Gelassenheit* — no where is the phenomenonological paradox of human accountability and human helplessness more poignantly or profoundly encountered than in Luther's own descriptions of the experience of despairing.

What is true at the individual level remains true at the level of corporate experience as well. Both Roman Catholic and Protestant traditions supplement their analyses of individual accountability with sensitivity to the broader social dimensions of the problem of despair. Rahner and Molinski do so by attending to the situational and structural factors which drive people to despair, involuntarily and non-culpably. Tillich does so by re-defining Sin (always in the singular) as a corporate state of brokenness, rather than an individually indictable deficiency or wrong-doing. From either perspective, the person who is despairing belongs to a broader matrix of community which shares both accountability for suffering and responsibility for becoming a mediating agency for the inbreaking of grace. We will return to this theme in greater detail at the close of this chapter.

Conclusion: The Catholic/Protestant Dialectic

In summary, both the Protestant focus on grace and the Roman Catholic focus on effort provide important insights for a theological approach to understanding despair and its healing, insights which ring with experiential authenticity. As we saw in Chapter One with both Isabel's and Celie's stories, the emergence from despair comes as a result of personal struggles for strength, discernment, and self-mastery; but it also comes as a result of personal "gifting" by the advent of insight, community, and assistance from unforeseeable sources. As we saw in Chapter Four with our typological analysis, there are levels in the "pyramid" of despairing where we *can* help ourselves; yet there are also profoundly experienced levels where we cannot seem to help ourselves at all. On the one hand, then, we do bear responsibility for certain features of our despairing: for narrowing our vision to acknowledge only the future of our own limited preconceptions; for closing ourselves off from the ministrations of others. Yet on the other hand, the wider human community must also assume responsibility: for perpetuating conditions which stifle our aspirations, for refusing to come to our aid, for squelching our abilities to reach out in vulnerable trust and openness to receiving healing.

This paradox of our own experiences is borne out by the dialectical counsel of Catholic and Protestant theological teaching. The spiritual direction of the "old moralists" exhorts us to *act*; the counterbalancing recommendation of Luther and Kierkegaard is to *trust*. Understood separately or simplistically, either course could lead to danger: to Pelagian activism and self-reliance ("I can do it all myself"); to predestinarian passivity and complacence ("I can't do anything, nor do I need to, for it all has been or will be done for me"). But together, they speak a salutary, if difficult, wisdom: act, but without presumption; trust, but without quietism. Or, in a more familiar phrasing of the dialectic: "Work out your own salvation with fear and trembling; for God is at work in you" (Phil 2:12–13).

The Christian Confession on Despairing: Crucifixion, Incarnation, Eschatological *Shalom*

Beyond this theological and phenomenological naming of the effort/grace dialectic which is woven through the divergent strands of Catholic and Protestant traditional teachings, the Christian confession as a whole has further wisdom to offer the person who is despairing. This wisdom focuses around three key moments in the Christian story: the crucifixion, the incarnation, and the promise of eschatological *shalom*. Each of these moments ultimately demands the perspective offered by the other two in order to avoid troubling distortions. Still, for the purposes of clarity and simplicity, we shall initially attend to them individually.

Crucifixion

It may seem curious to begin an account of the Christian story by focusing on the crucifixion rather than on birth narratives or creation accounts, either of which might appear more suitable as a rendering of "the beginning." Yet, there is a strong sense in which Christianity as a drama of human redemption pivots upon the reconciling moment of divine suffering on a cross. Certainly, any theology which intends to be sensitive to the reality of despairing must find its starting point and its centerpiece in the passion — and the compassion — which are here made manifest.

For, a focus on the cross discloses what a discussion of the sinfulness of despair can otherwise too easily overlook — namely, the fact that despair is an integral part of being human, a dimension of our humanness that even God Godself did not spurn to embrace. Too much talk about either the impiety or the pathology of despairing can cause us to negate our own experience — to deny the real painfulness of our living, to attempt to smooth it over with whatever palliatives come most readily to hand, be they drugs or material possessions, televangelistic theologies of prosperity or sugar-coated political pronouncements that we are living in a "kinder, gentler, nation." But if we dare to look into the features of the Crucified One, we can no longer countenance such travesties. Rejection and loneliness, anguish and God-forsakenness, the betrayal of hopes and the dashing of dreams — all of these appear as realities in our lived humanity, and in the lived humanity of Jesus as the Christ. To pretend any different is to fall prey to a docetic heresy: one which claims that Jesus merely *seemed* to be human; that he did not really suffer; that human suffering as such does not matter, but only the gnostic redemption of the unfettered spirit. Counter to this heresy, theologian Dorothée Soelle proclaims: "It is clear that Christianity makes an overwhelming affirmation of suffering, far stronger than many other world views that do not have as their center the symbol of the cross."[9]

William Lynch parallels Soelle's affirmation in his insightful and pastoral book, *Images of Hope*. Describing a misguided Christian perspective on despair which has forgotten the centrality of the crucifixion, he writes:

> I have heard a chaplain in a mental hospital harangue the sick to the effect that they need not worry about any other human failings, but that if they have the feeling of hopelessness or despair they should panic, rush to the chapel, and throw themselves before the altar, beseeching the forgiveness and mercy of God.[10]

The author of such a harangue has obviously listened too simplistically to the words of the "old moralists" when they label despair the "unforgivable sin against the Holy Ghost." True, from a Catholic analysis, despair as the voluntary renunciation of trust in God by an otherwise healthy and trustful person can be a sinful act; true, from a Protestant perspective, even involuntary despair can be the evidence and the outgrowth of a pervasive state of brokenness, estrangement, and Sin. Nevertheless, both Catholic and Protestant approaches to despair must be infused by a deeper understanding that the anguish of despairing also stands as a tragic part of the human condition — a part which should not receive undialectical condemnation, because God deigns to lift it up into the divine embrace through the outstretched arms of Jesus on the cross.

Thus, under the sign of the cross, Lynch helps us in searching out positive dimensions of despairing. He is not advocating the pretentious and melodramatic "spleen" so prized by the nineteenth century and so satirized by Kierkegaard. He is, however, affirming a phenomenon akin to the *bona tristitia* which figures in the patristic and scholastic traditions, and to the "beautiful despair" which characterizes some of Luther's experiences. In the history of Christian thought, such good or beautiful despair is seen to serve a chastening function: it reminds us of our shortcomings and our vulnerability; it urges us to humility and reliance upon grace.

In Lynch's more modern language, the experience of despair is also seen to serve a significant, chastening function: it curtails the destructive aspirations of our "absolutizing" or "fantastic" imagination. Under the sway of this faculty, we create superhuman ideals for ourselves. Like Isabel, we yearn for relationships in which those we love will not die. Like Kierkegaard's "willful" despairer, we yearn for mastery and perfection, in defiance of all our personal limitations. Despair, in fact, can help us by forcing us to cut such presumptuous aspirations down to size.

Lynch specifies the valuable lesson to be learned from such pedagogy:

> The plain fact for all of us is that many things are without hope, many people we are inclined to depend on cannot give hope, and many isolated moments or periods of life do not themselves contain hope. . . . Hope is not absolute in its range. Part of reality belongs to hopelessness (54).

If we can learn to admit this forthrightly, humbly accepting the realistic limits of the human condition, we will make significant strides in moving away from the fragile blend of naiveteé, arrogance, and blinkered idealism that so often disguises itself as human, and as Christian, hoping. In the throes of such false hope, we are too prone to give up on *everything* if some one thing for which we have wished does not come true. Despair can school us away from this into true hoping — into the tempered and toughened attitude which persists when the actual parameters of hopelessness have been acknowledged. Paradoxically, owning up to the inevitable presence of despair in some portions of our lives can relieve us of the further despair which appears when hope tries to "absolutize" its range.

For Lynch, part of acknowledging the reality of hopelessness includes acknowledging the degree to which we are not always able to "help ourselves." At the close of Chapter Four, we touched upon his observation about the limits of the "private imagination." He carries this observation forward in his discussion — so opposite to Solomon's contentions — of the realities of human helplessness. While Lynch's focus is on the pathology of mental illness, he professes that this experience "is only a painful reflection of [our] universal helplessness in the face of [our] destiny" (76). "I propose," he writes, "that the sick person *is* really helpless, and that there is nothing more human than to be helpless" (77). But to say that we are "beyond the point of self-help" is not to say that we are beyond help altogether. Rather, it is to say that we are at the point where we are dependent upon — and ripe to receive — help from another. We need the assistance of another's imagination to supplement the constrictedness of our own. We need the assurance of another's presence to sustain us when we have reached the limits of our own abilities to cope.

It is here that the moment of crucifixion in the Christian story once again shows its salience for a theological understanding of despair. Not only does the cross validate the reality of suffering, teaching us that in this world it is unrealistic and destructive to hope blindly for all things. Moreover, the cross shows us the willingness of the One who is ultimate in being, meaning, and value to *be with us* (Emmanuel) in our suffering, to dwell with us at the deepest pitch of our despairing. This gift of presence does not "make everything better" in the *deus ex machina* fashion of Greek and Roman drama. It does, however, offer us the strength and solace which come from knowing that nothing can ultimately separate us from the empowering love of the divine *com*-passion.

Eschatological *Shalom*

From the center point of the cross, we can look both backward to the incarnation, life, and ministry of Jesus, and forward to the time of wholeness and healing which his life foreshadows. Because it is the latter, eschatological moment of the Christian story which is the more likely to neglect its vital relationship to the crucifixion, we shall look at it first, while the image of the cross is still before our eyes.

Eschatological teachings tend toward triumphalism: in the fullness of time, they tell us, God and all the Heavenly Regiment will sweep down from the clouds to establish a reign of blessing.

No matter what the ills of the present, all will eventually be made well. Such teachings have had much to say to despair throughout the Christian ages. They have labeled it blasphemous for seeming to doubt God's power to effect such a transformation. Like the chaplain in Lynch's description, they have harangued the despairing to rush to the chapel and throw themselves before the altar, beseeching forgiveness for the sin of disbelieving.

There is both wisdom and danger to such an eschatological orientation. The danger lies in our propensity for neglecting the fact that the God who is to bring about the longed-for transformation is the same God whose approach to redeeming human evil was to suffer and die upon a cross. Eschatology viewed from the vantage point of the crucifixion eschews the temptations of easy triumphalism. Grand and imposing "fix-it" schemes are not part of the divine repertoire. Not a dramatic show of force, not a *deus ex machina* intervention, but rather a steadfast and long-suffering process of wooing: God wins the world to blessedness through the persistent persuasiveness of a compassionate presence which, ultimately, no power will be able to resist.[11]

In the face of so much penultimate resistance, however, to be convinced of the final victory of this wooing power is necessarily a matter of faith, not of sight. Such faith is nurtured by the stories, liturgies, and symbols of Christianity; it is shaped by a rich history of communal imagining which supplements and sustains the constricted resources of our "private imaginations." The wisdom of the eschatological orientation, counterbalancing its triumphalistic danger, lies in the healing and whole-making assurances it offers — assurances like those which "inspirited" Isabel and Celie, assurances like those which empower each of us to keep moving through the pain of our lives with courage and hopeful conviction.

Precisely what are these assurances? For what may we legitimately — which is to say, non-triumphally — hope? The "venturesome faith" of a cross-centered Christian eschatology suggests five things. We may legitimately hope for God's *presence* with us in our suffering, as the source our inbreaking courage. We may legitimately hope for God's *partisanship* with us when we struggle to create wholeness, reconciliation, justice, right-eousness, peace — all of which are rendered in the Hebrew word *shalom*. We may legitimately hope for God's *preservation* of every being, moment, act, and person which contributes to the process of *shalom*-making. We may legitimately hope for God's *promise* that all these acts, in their preservation, will and do contribute to an eternal wellspring of blessing, which will over-flow upon us in the fullness of time. We may legitimately hope for God's good *pleasure* that the divine project of wooing the world will ultimately be completed. At this point, the language of myth and poetry must take over: and justice will roll down like waters; tears will be wiped from crying eyes; lions and lambs, children and asps, will frolic and lie down together; and upon God's Holy Mountain, all will be peace.

If the stories and symbols, the poetry and liturgy, the theol-ogy and mythology of the Christian imagination teach us that we may legitimately and, indeed, eagerly hope for these five things, then they simultaneously conspire to give us a visuali-zing framework with significant implications for our under-standing of despair. From the perspective shaped by such a framework, no matter how rational and warranted despair may seem to be under the onus of present circumstances, any capit-ulation to ultimate despair comes to appear as irrational, unjus-tified. For, from the perspective of Christian eschatology, we cannot and must not foreclose on the possibility that God is perennially with us in our suffering, winning and wooing the forces that surround us into "doing a new thing," offering us gifts and gracious potentialities for healing which move beyond the confines of our immediately despair-ridden imaginings.

It is within the orientation provided by an eschatological vision that despair has primarily earned its designation by the "old moralists" of Christianity as sinful. Yet, paradoxically, even within such an angle of vision, despair can also be appropriated to serve a fruitful pedagogical function. Robert Roberts, whose work on emotions and moods proved so instructive in Chapter Four, once again offers insightful assistance. He writes:

> A suffering can become a viscerally moving symbol of the present world's unfitness to satisfy my deepest needs. It can become a reminder, more vivid than any mere *word* of truth,

that the present passing world is not my home — that I am a sojourner, a passer through.[12]

When I am stunned by the slamming of doors, the sundering of relationships, the shattering of dreams — at such moments, I can "viscerally" awaken to the price of investing too much confidence in the ephemeral. The failure of proximate hopes — as Kierkegaard knew so well — can cast me onto the eternal. The inability of this passing world to satisfy and sustain me, an inability which becomes palpable in despair, can school me toward the hope for an ultimate and indestructible wholeness where the restless heart will at last find rest.

Still, we must be very careful about how we speak of such an eschatological wisdom. Roberts himself is sensitive to this fact. In addition to the danger of triumphalism (God will swoop in from the clouds and "fix" everything) lies the danger of escapism (life may be miserable now, but everything will be happy in the hereafter). Both dangers share a gnostic propensity to negate the processes of the present world. Again, we must look at eschatology through the lens of crucifixion. The cross teaches us — poignantly, painfully — that benediction comes, not in the evasion of suffering, but in its embrace: in the tribulations of the self, and in afflictions borne to alleviate the suffering of others. Further, we must look at eschatology through the lens of the incarnation. For, the embodied existence of Jesus as the Christ teaches us that even with all of its perils and disappointments, life in this world is an arena which God has chosen to indwell and to sanctify. Or, as Roberts concludes:

> . . . sufferings can become a powerful aid in getting the right perspective on the prospects which the world holds out. The Christian does not despise those prospects, as one might who did not believe that God created [and indwelled] this present world; but he learns from his sufferings not to put his deepest heart into those prospects, and to reserve it instead for what is promised in the gospel (103–104).

It is the balance — learning not to overvalue, yet also not to despise, the present world — which emerges in the conjunction of eschatology and incarnation. To clarify this balance, we must now examine the latter doctrine in its turn.

Incarnation

In approaching the relevance of the doctrine of the incarnation for an understanding of despair within the confessional teachings of Christianity, we would do well to "incarnate" our own investigations, turning to the specificity of an embodied example. The story of Celie which we unfolded in Chapter One provides us with an appropriate setting. Since her childhood, Celie has been beaten down emotionally and physically: raped repeatedly by her alleged father; torn away from her children; deprived of an education; given away in marriage to a man who batters and abuses her; separated from the one friend she has in her sister Nettie; crushed under the burdens of poverty and racism and sexism and understandably low self-esteem. Bereft of pleasures and companionship, exhausted of all except the meagerest of energies required to survive — Celie lives in a world from which the promises of "eschatological *shalom*" seem remote to a cruel degree.

If we can travel in our imaginations on a pastoral call to Celie's world — or to the world of so many like her who live in neighborhoods not so very far from our own — what might we say out of the heart of our Christian convictions? Do we tell her that her despair of realizing various earthly hopes — for companionship, for safety, for dignity — is misplaced? Do we tell her that any such despair is sinful, that she should be able to minimize and master it by the disciplined virtue of hope for a heavenly resolution? Unfortunately, this is likely to be the approach taken by persons who detach the doctrine of eschatology from its kindred doctrines of incarnation and crucifixion. But such detachment is not only insensitive. It is also, regardless of its intentions or pretensions, singularly unChristian.

Christianity, instead, holds two key convictions in dynamic tension: the eschatological conviction that the brokenness of this world cannot finally defeat the blessedness to come in the ultimate *shalom* of God; but also, the incarnational conviction that this very world, in all its brokenness and tragedy, remains a chosen locus for God's reconciling activity. To discount the pains of the present — even in the light of an eschatological vision — fundamentally distorts Christianity. Jesus assuredly does not discount suffering. His particular ministry to the poor, the outcast, the diseased and the disabled attests to Christianity's abiding concern for this-worldly reality. Solidly grounding his life and ministry, Jesus' very *being* as Christ incarnate, God in the flesh, hallows the bodily, the human, and the here and now in such a fashion that any facile utterance of eschatological promises sounds as a gnostic perversion. The good news of the incarnation thus means, in a radical sense, that God's healing concern does not limit itself to eternal and spiritual reconciliation. Rather, it also reaches out to encompass very proximate and palpable concerns, as they may be expressed in despair over poverty or powerlessness, disease or dehumanization.

What, then, do we say to Celie — or to so many women and men like her in the despair of their daily living? First, it seems to me, if we have attended to the gospel of the incarnation, we tell her that she is, in measure, *right* in her despairing. As ones who believe that God created and indwelled this present world, we must assure her that the things for which she longs — physical security, rest, companionship, appreciation, meaning — are both healthy and valid. Her despair is the voice of a vital and legitimate protest that matters are not as they should be. Neither are her desires for earthly fulfillments misplaced, nor is there anything about her as an individual which particularly deserves their deprivation. From the perspective of the incarnation, her despair is neither sin nor the wages of sin — except in its painful testimony to how far short the whole present world has fallen from the intended justice of God.

Even within this fallen world, however, an incarnational theology insists on the existence of certain curative and restorative potentials. A significant measure of healing comes through the flesh, as both Martin Luther and Robert Burton remind us. Of this gospel, Shug Avery proves to be the preacher extraordinaire. From sexual pleasures to the color purple in a field, Shug proclaims the winsome presence of a divine reality so desirous of our love and contentment that "It always making little surprises and springing them on us when us least expect" (178). If we can let ourselves relax into the sustaining riches of that reality, we can find resources of patience and even of joyous celebration which work to keep total despair from infiltrating the vital reservoirs of our terrestrial hope.

The insight which Alice Walker voices through Shug is close kindred to an insight which Mary Gordon voices through Isabel, and which William Lynch affirms in his philosophical and psychological analysis of hoping. Like Celie, Isabel comes to an epiphany of healing which resonates with the significance of the incarnation. "Christ had suffered in the body, and I too had a body," she affirms. "I knew it false but capable of astonishing pleasures." After a lengthy retreat into the slow suicide of despairing dullness, these words finally mark Isabel's emergence: ". . . it was not death I wanted. It was life, and the body, which had been given to me for my pleasure, and the love of those whom loving was a pleasure" (247).

Or Lynch, approaching the incarnational question from the opposite direction. "It is, in fact, highly probable," he observes, "that people who do not attend to detail are poor in hope." Such neglect of detail he terms "contempt," going so far as to label contempt as hope's "opposite" (33). To be contemptuous of detail is to be anti-incarnational in our outlook. The contemptuous element in despair is that which focuses so exclusively on one provocation to hopelessness that it neglects all the myriad of smaller but still significant, "incarnate" voices which summon and sustain the surge of hope within us. Even when we are in the throes of a particularly painful situation, we can still be uplifted by the "astonishing pleasures" which Isabel mentions, by the beauties and surprises of the divinity whom Shug Avery celebrates. Mauve-red sunrises, hot coffee, favorite music, unexpected greetings from a friend far away: none of these small pleasures will resolve the difficulties troubling us, that is true. But that is not the point. Rather, the point is that attending to such humble — and fundamentally incarnational — *details* can fortify us to find live worth living, at however tacit a level, while we wait with courageous patience for the advent of a more substantial resolution.

Of course, such pleasures have their limits, and terrestrial hope seems inevitably to fall prey to bitter disappointments. At such moments, the teachings of eschatology again take on importance. This world is indeed one of God's gracious indwelling, but it is also one which groans in travail, awaiting a future consummation. Earthly events do satisfy, but their satisfactions prove preliminary, unpredictable, and passing. The ephemeral nature of secular satisfactions can awaken us vividly to the need for something more than this finite and fallen existence to animate a life which moves beyond the roller-coaster of hope and hopelessness or the deadened plane of resignation. Such animation can come powerfully through the Christian confession of faith in an eschatological fulfillment. If we dare to venture this faith — and it remains a venture rather than a mathematical certainty — then we recognize that those blessed moments when new resources of courage, patience, and hopefulness unexpectedly well up within us stand as joyous foretastes of a time to come "when every tear will be wiped from crying eyes." If we venture this faith, then we dare to look at our experiences through a visualizing framework in which final despair becomes inappropriate — no matter how appropriate it may have appeared in the lone illumination of our this-worldly prospects. Still, it seems only fitting to speak of this final "inappropriateness" only after the real pains, and pleasures, of a person's concrete situation have been acknowledged — even as it is fitting to rejoice on Easter morning only after the Hosannahs of Palm Sunday and the tragedy of Good Friday have been genuinely lived through.

What, then, does Christianity have to say to the Celies of this world? Robert Roberts has called us to a balanced perspective: a faithful attitude which "neither over-nor underestimates [our] earthly prospects" (95). To cultivate such an attitude requires hearty self-discipline. Yet, the conquest of despairing demands a dual dialectic — not simply that of eschatology and incarnation, but also, as we have seen, that of exertion and grace. Writing on *The Problem of Pain* within Christian theology, C. S. Lewis has offered an invaluable observation: "When pain is to be borne, a little courage helps more than much knowledge, [and] a little human sympathy more than much courage."[13] Human sympathy — human compassion which re-incarnates the loving and co-suffering presence of God revealed in Jesus as the Christ — comes to us as an empowering and gracious gift. For the Celies of the world, better than all the consolations of an eschatological vision and all the reassurances of an incarnational theology would be a community of persons committed to acting out that very theology — a community committed in concrete ways to carrying forward the confessional conviction that God's love seeks to become real to human beings through the mediations and ministrations of human flesh.

Such ministrations need not be monumental. After all, when God became flesh in Jesus, that act offered no miraculous, *deus ex machina* triumph which single-handedly overturned the political, economic, and social structures provocative of human despairing. Likewise, our ministry need not attempt miraculous and triumphal acts of "rescue." God in Jesus empowered people to work within their own means and freedoms to bring about life-alterations. The spirit of Christ in us works to empower those whom we encounter through a similar ministry of compassionate presence. Small gestures — offering child care, transportation, a listening ear, a warming touch — in the moment of need, assume a gracious magnitude.

In traditional theological language, of course, the community of persons who minister in such ways, making manifest God's continuing and caring incarnation, is known as "the body of Christ." Any group which does not so minister, regardless of its professions of faith, is not worthy of the name; any group which does so minister deserves the appellation, whether it chooses to claim such for itself or not (and there may be valid reasons for choosing not to do so). But this assertion begins to move us away from the doctrines of crucifixion, eschatology, and incarnation, and into the doctrine of ecclesiology. More generally, this move leads us into the third guiding issue of this concluding chapter: How does the traditional Christian story shape itself to address the particular needs of the present day? The first distinctive element of such shaping has to do with an emphasis on confessionalism rather than on Christocentric exclusivism — an element clearly connected to the type of ecclesiology alluded to above. The connections will become clearer as we progress through the final section of our contemporary construction of a Christian theology of despair.

Contemporary Emphases:
Confessionalism, Courage, and Communal Responsibility

Confessionalism

To say that any community which ministers to human needs constitutes a portion of "the body of Christ" is to fly in the face of certain traditional assumptions. Primarily, it is to fly in the face of assumptions about the primacy of naming the name of Jesus in order to be either saved or saving. Christocentrism — insistence on the explicit profession of Jesus Christ as savior — has dominated the history of teachings on despair within the Christian tradition. As we saw with Kierkegaard at the close of Chapter Three, assumptions have abounded that the only person safe from the ultimate ravages of despair is the "true Christian": "To be sharply observant of this sickness constitutes the Christian's advantage over the natural man [*sic*]," Kierkegaard proclaims, and "to be healed is the Christian's bliss."[14]

Such assumptions have lost some of their credibility in the contemporary context. In a world whose cultural and religious pluralism have become increasingly evident, to state that only "true Christians" are freed from despair sounds presumptuous indeed. In a world where professedly Christian nations have contributed to sowing widespread despair among non-Christian peoples through acts of political imperialism, economic exploitation, and genocidal holocaust, the problem is further compounded. In such a world, it seems more fitting to eschew any proclamations which smack of theological exclusivism. Rather than listen for the explicit faith professions of people or populations in order to rule on their degree of susceptibility to despair or amenability to its healing, would we not do better to attend to the specific life experiences of such people — to the strains of discouragement or of resilient hopefulness which sound through the tenor of their living?

This is the approach of confessionalism. A confessional theology does not attempt to make absolutist and universal pronouncements. Rather, it makes bold to speak in the first person, to utter its own "confession" of faith and of personal experience.[15] Using a confessional approach to a theology of despair, I speak of my own struggles with discouragement and depression; I seek to articulate the sources which offer sustenance within my own daily existence. I listen intently to the stories of kindred spirits — be they contemporary or historical, actual or fictional companions in the struggle (Isabel and Celie, Paul Tillich and Robert Burton, Father William Lynch or Father Daniel of Cassian's *Collationes Patrum*). Wherever or whenever I see healing take place in the lives of such persons — in moments of epiphany, in acts of community intervention, in inbreakings of "the courage to be" — I celebrate those victories. In the vocabulary of my own faith tradition, I may speak of them as indications of God's continuing incarnation, as foretastes of God's intended *shalom*, as evidences that the Body of Christ is ministering to the needs of its members. But I do not insist that others use this vocabulary, unless it strikes up resonances in the depths of their own being. While steady in my faith commitments, and convinced of their value in helping to open up and articulate salutary dimensions within my own experience, my confessional approach urges humility about translating those commitments into the faith perspectives of other people. Given the contemporary context of religious pluralism and incipient steps toward interfaith dialogue, such humility appears more appropriate and more promising than the presumptuousness of Christocentric exclusivism.

Courage

The preceding counsel of humility carries two implications. On the one hand, humility can school us in sensitivity to other people. No longer preoccupied with "selling" them on the fact that our solution to despairing is the uniquely effective remedy, we learn to listen better: we attend more genuinely to their pain; we discern more appreciatively the sources of hope and wholeness which animate their lives.

On the other hand, humility can also school us in greater sensitivity with ourselves. The "old moralists" knew the healthful value of paring down our exalted expectations. Their linkage of *desperatio* and *praesumptio* echoes in William Lynch's counsel to chasten the excesses of our "absolutizing" imaginations. To wish indiscriminately for all things lands us in trouble. We become easily discouraged; we grow sour and judgmental — antipathetic rather than sympathetic toward ourselves and toward those around us. In its countering of such destructive dynamics, humility is healing. It restores us to patience. And patience is a first step toward a tenacious hopefulness which casts out despair.

Yet, for all its wisdom, this counsel of humility also has its dangers. Like so many of the teachings of Christianity — like exertion and grace, like eschatology and incarnation — it must be understood dialectically. Humility has been recommended as healing for despair — rightly so. But humility cannot stand as the lone remedial virtue. *Fortitudo* has also been extolled, especially in the writings of John Cassian. This leads us to the second contemporary emphasis of our constructive theology. In an age of mass communications, in which we have become increasingly aware of all the ravages and inhumanities that torment our planet; in a nuclear age, in which we are slowly waking up to the horrific threat that all life as we know it may be destroyed — in such an age, humility alone is not what is needed. We already feel dwarfed by the principalities and powers that surround us. Further chastening becomes dangerous. We need invigorating; we need empowering; we need inspiriting. In the wise and rigorous counsel of the "old moralists" of Christianity: we need *courage*.

Ancient wisdom meets modern inquiry in surprising and illuminating ways at this juncture. One of the critiques at the forefront of recent feminist theology has been of a tendency within Christianity to focus so exclusively on the predominantly "masculine" sins of overweening self-assertion that we neglect the energy-sapping sins of self-abnegation.[16] Despair clearly stands as one of the latter sins. Despair concludes that I can do nothing in the face of overwhelming circumstances before me; it further concludes that I can expect no real help from any thing or anybody. Such conclusions do not need humility for their cure; in fact, an undialectical dose of humility lies at the root of the problem.

It is surprising that Kierkegaard overlooks this point— surprising in that his diagnosis of the "feminine" despairs of weakness is so astute. But he does not pause in his depiction of the various "sicknesses unto death" to recommend remedial measures for this frail failure in the will to be a self. Rather, he proceeds immediately down his typology, diagnosing the corollary despairs of presumptuous and willful defiance. Only thereafter does he propose a cure — and it is humility, rather more suited to the latter than to the former of the two diseases of the spirit.

Few thinkers in contemporary Christian writings on sin and healing do much better. Judith Plaskow has written a compelling critique in which she faults Reinhold Niebuhr and Paul Tillich for a similarly "masculinist" bias. Niebuhr she criticizes for a complete neglect of the feminine — a neglect resulting from his central and Augustinian focus on sin as the prideful concentration upon self rather than God. Tillich she criticizes less for neglect of the feminine; his definition of Sin as a state of separation (which we have seen earlier in this chapter) applies equally well to men or to women. His deficiency, rather, lies in a failure of concrete application.[17]

Plaskow — as many other feminists — would have theological phrases like "Sin as separation" and "grace as 'the courage to be'" show their salience for concrete situations of human living. Thus, Sin becomes the "separation" of human beings from one another in exploitive divisions of race, sexuality, or class, while courage becomes the energy to do battle against the injustices of such divisions. Sin becomes the "separation" that deprives people like Celie of a feeling of value, while courage sounds in the sheer tenacity of her affirmation: "All I know how to do is stay alive" (26). Sin is the capitulation that decides one person's efforts make no difference; courage is the stubbornness to persist, even in the face of limitations and of self-doubts. Courage, *fortitudo*, entails the conquest of demons, whether they exist within the self or in the principalities of oppression operative in the world at large. Cassian and other "old moralists" knew of the concrete dimensions of such combat, and their insights — curiously anticipatory of the feminists — can once again serve us well.

The construction of a contemporary theological perspective on despair thus beckons us to the consideration of a new/old model of Christian virtue. It is a model which de-emphasizes certain present-day assumptions about what it means to lead a Christian life — assumptions about the practice of patriotism, giving unquestioning allegiance to God and country (often curiously conflated with one another); assumptions about the practice of "family values" (sexual orthodoxy, fidelity, respect for a hierarchy of obedience to command). To suggest the de-emphasis of such values is not to denigrate the importance of loyalty to our countries or to those persons with whom we are joined by bonds of blood or vowed commitments. It is, however, to suggest that such loyalties are subsidiary to the principal call of Christian morality. This principal call re-emphasizes the wisdom of the "old moralists." They taught that the primary virtue of Christianity inheres in an unswerving passion, not for family or homeland, but for God — a passion embodied in various ways: in a life committed to sharing that passion in prayer for and ministry toward the needs of others; in a life of pertinacious rejoicing, celebrating the gifts of incarnation and anticipating a consummation when God's fullness will be all in all; in a life of faith, hope, and love — the theological virtues — to be sure; but also in a life which works to cultivate in itself the steadying presence of the "cardinal" virtues: patience, justice, temperance, courage. Amid the trials and temptations to despair which engulf us in our contemporary context, it seems apt to suggest that the greatest of these is courage.[18]

Communal Responsibility

This new/old model of Christian virtue has corporate as well as individual implications. While I can — and there are times when I must — be courageous on my own, the Christian model of courage is not finally that of the Stoic individual, facing the vicissitudes of life and the inevitability of death with a steely equanimity. Rather, it is that of the *koinonia* community — the Body of Christ (whether it chooses to call itself this or no) whose fellowship in intended to *en-courage* its members. Such fellowship expresses itself incarnationally: it feeds the hungry, clothes the naked, treats the outcast with human dignity. Such fellowship also expresses itself in the richness of eschatological imagining: to the aching, the lonely, the aggrieved, it holds up a life-giving vision, filling and fortifying the reservoirs of hope run dry in their private imaginations. William James says of courage that it is "contagious," springing up in contact with the courage of another.[19] The Body of Christ, however it be named, exists to spread the contagion: to infect and infuse its members with a resilience sufficient to withstanding the crucifixions of daily living.

This stress on fellowship, on the corporate upbuilding of courage and hopefulness, highlights the third distinctive emphasis of a contemporary theology of despairing: an emphasis on communal responsibility rather than on individual redemption from sin. For much of the history of ideas of despair, the focus was more typically the opposite. Earlier preoccupations with *desperatio* — particularly in the medieval penitential literature — concerned themselves centrally with despair of the forgiveness of sins. Convictions of guilt and unworthiness haunted the confessionals; the object of such despair was the *bonum divinum* — the goodness of God. To despair of one's forgiveness was to doubt this goodness, to disbelieve that God was merciful. Despairing over one's sin thus blasphemously compounded one's sin — as Søren Kierkegaard later reiterated in analyzing the convolutions of "despairing over despair."

In the twentieth century, however, this degree of intense preoccupation with the forgiveness of sins has appreciably waned. As Tillich diagnoses it, our modern anxiety is less characteristically that of guilt and condemnation and more typically that of emptiness and meaninglessness.[20] In this age between two holocausts, the Nazi and the nuclear (as Sallie McFague has named it),[21] we worry less over the redemption of our souls in some otherworldly future and more over whether or not there will be an ongoing future for *this* world. We worry less over the personal meaning of our peccadilloes in some divine record book of salvation and damnation and more over whether or not there can be any ultimate meaning for the travail of our lives and of cosmic history. In this preeminently modern context, the *bonum divinum* remains a powerful, albeit often unspoken, object of our despairing. But the "divine good" of which we despair is not focally that of mercy for individual sinners. Rather, it is that of God's gracious ability to bring about ultimate *shalom* for the whole groaning creation.

As human creatures within this creation, we are not merely participants in the groaning. We are also partners with God — in whose image we are created — for the task of *shalom*-making. This side of God's *shalom*, situations of sensed powerlessness still drive many to despair: battered women, like Celie, who feel unable to leave their spouses because they have no job skills, no social network, no means of moral or financial support; grieving persons, like Isabel, who feel unable to face into the future because, no matter what they do, everyone they love will be torn away from them through separation and loss. When any such people are in despair, feeling politically or psychologically disempowered, it becomes incumbent upon us, as members of one Body, to offer help — to act as encouraging and empowering. In this, our corporate responsibility for bearing one another's burdens, we discover the most significant connotations of a revitalized understanding of despair as Sin. The issue no longer focuses so heavily on individual culpability and need for redemption. *All* of us have sinned and fallen short; all of us are implicated in the hurts of one another. But, even further, just as we cannot redeem our own fallenness, so we cannot be expected to remedy our own despairing. We are dependent upon one another, as agents of grace, in both the political and psychological arenas of our living.

In the political arena, there are specific things we can do to minimize or eliminate occasions of despair. Because so much despair derives from a sense of powerlessness, we can act as empowerers: helping the illiterate to read, helping the unemployed to learn skills, helping the abused to discover inner resources of self-esteem and resilience. So many provocations to despair come from types of brokenness that we could fix, were we to apply our energies in the appropriate directions. As the "pyramid" of Chapter Four indicated, the levels of frustration/despair/depression all interpenetrate, and the healing of one is not finally possible without attention to the others. Thus, despair cannot be fully addressed in isolation from efforts to rectify circumstances which thwart and frustrate people's legitimate longings. At this level, there are ways in which we can act to help ourselves, and further ways in which we can become helpers of others. In our new/old model of Christian virtue, in fact, it becomes imperative that we do so. If despair is Sin and we are exhorted not to lead any of our brothers or sisters into paths of temptation, so we are liable for not abandoning any of our sisters or brothers in hopeless situations. A contemporary theological approach to despair thus calls us to become actively and constructively political.

In the psychological arena, as well, we are called to action, ranging from ministries of presence to medical intervention. At times, despair truly does issue from sickness — from psychological or physiological enervation. There are conditions under which the pain of living pierces so deeply that all we can do is ache and yearn for an ending. There are occasions when the circumstances of our lives send us reeling from blows of seemingly unendurable misfortunes. At such times, despair readily shades into the lowest and most global reaches of the "pyramid" taxonomy: depression. Depression of clinical or pathological dimensions requires medical treatment.[22] Depression of less entrenched or enduring proportions cries out for the simple therapies of friendship and compassion. "Doing something" to help may entail doing nothing more than being present for and with one another. It is hard to be hopeful alone; it is not good that any of us should have to be so. Despair impels us to acknowledge our individual limitations and our personal interconnectedness: to let ourselves be cared for, to activate ourselves to care for one another. Communal responsibility for communal care and whole-making highlights a theology of despair attuned to the needs of spirits, selves, and societies in the present day.

Conclusion

Is despair, then, a sin or a sickness? Our investigations have implied both answers at various points. Or more precisely, our investigations have led us to the conclusion that despair is neither sin nor sickness *per se*, but rather a *symptom* of both. Despair testifies poignantly to the brokenness in our world, brokenness in both political and personal arenas. Sometimes life patently hurts us; other times we simply hurt and do not know why. In either situation, despair can serve us as a stringent teacher — schooling us in humility, sensitivity, and courage; refining our abilities to wait with patience and persistence for the inbreaking of healing grace. In a curious sense, despair can even become our friend. It saves us from a facile naiveté which skims over the surface of life, never risking to feel or to probe too deeply; it saves us from a flat resignation which retreats from experience, never risking to invest too much. Despair forces us to probe, and it attests through its pain to the intensity of our caring. As Thomas Aquinas suggested, despair derives its animation from an ardent desire for the good. Such desire is precious and worth preserving. Buried within it lie the seeds of its own transformation: the person who dares to despair possesses a tensile spirit which can learn to brave the even more radical venture of hoping.

To speak of despair as teacher and potential friend is not, however, to make light of the experience. Despair hurts: our own, and that of other persons to whom we are bonded as fellow creatures. It figures among the palpable tragedies of life this side of the Garden of Eden. It sears our heart and fills our eyes with tears, as at so many subsequent garden scenes of our human living: "Must I drink of this cup?"; "Could you not stay awake with me but a little while?"; "They have taken my Beloved away, and I do not know where they have laid him."

Still, at least in the context of Christian teaching and conviction, despair does not deserve the final word. The confession of Christianity proclaims that deeper than despair lies a context of ultimate blessing. Frederick Buechner refers to this context as "the laughter of things beyond the tears of things."[23] He does not speak of "the laughter of things apart from the tears of things," or "the laughter of things in neglect of the tears." Rather, he speaks of a laughter which sounds beyond the tears, after persistence and courage and inbreaking grace have enabled us to move through them and out onto the other side. Tears and laughter, like incarnation and eschatology, like exertion and grace, like courage and humility — like hope and despair — move in a dialectical spiral, in a rhythm of dancing. It is a dance of cosmic — and ultimately, of comic — dimensions. It is a dance which calls before us once again the scene of Isabel's epiphany.

Climbing the stairs to her darkened room, slowed by the weight of her despair yet simmering with the energy of newly-released anger, Isabel finds herself recalling a phrase and a story from her Catholic childhood. Mary, the friend and devoted companion of Jesus, has anointed his feet with a jar of costly spikenard — so much of it that the whole house is filled with the fragrance. Judas rebukes her: Why was this ointment not sold to raise money for the poor? Jesus silences him in a surprising and easily misinterpreted fashion: "The poor you always have with you," he says, "but you do not always have me."

Isabel's healing epiphany comes in a sudden realization of the meaning of this statement. "The poor you always have with you." The multiple pains of life in a fallen world will continually surround us: poverty, injustice, prejudice, the failure of aspirations, the death of people we love. This side of the Garden of Eden and this side of the fullness of God's *shalom*, despair we will always have with us. Yet that realization does not culminate the story. Jesus' response to Judas continues: "You do not always have me." Jesus' time in the flesh is limited — as is our own. Incarnate moments are as precious as they are passing. We must learn to dance while the Beloved is in our midst.

Despair we will always have with us: that is the tragic moment in the dialectic of our living. Yet the Beloved is also among us — in the incarnate presence of our neighbors, in the stories of our communal imaginings, in the epiphanies which break in upon us as gifts and foretastes of a beckoning fullness beyond. This is the moment of high comedy. The Christian confession speaks to both elements of the dialectic, if we listen with discerning attention. Despair can attune us to the rich counterpoint between the promises of Christianity and the deepest yearnings of our spirits. Hearing echoes of this counter-point, even though our heartsickness may linger, we can learn to laugh and to hope and to be courageous together. In the embrace of the incarnation, we can learn to dance.

NOTES

Introduction

1. William Lynch, *Images of Hope: Imagination as Healer of the Hopeless* (Notre Dame: University of Notre Dame Press, 1965), p. 21.

2. Henry David Thoreau, *Walden, Or Life in the Woods* (New York: Libra Collection, 1960), p. 7.

Chapter 1

1. Throughout this chapter, page references will be indicated parenthetically in the text for the following two works: Mary Gordon, *Final Payments* (New York: Random House, 1978), and Alice Walker, *The Color Purple* (New York: Washington Square Press, 1983 [New York: Simon and Schuster, 1982]).

Chapter 2

1. For a discussion of the vice lists found in Aristotle's *Nicomachean Ethics* (II,II) and *Eudemian Ethics* (II, III, iv), see Reinhard Kuhn, *The Demon of Noontide: Ennui in Western Literature* (Princeton: Princeton University Press, 1976), p. 19.

2. See Aristotle, *Problemata Physica*, III, I, identified in Kuhn, p. 19, and translated and discussed in Raymond Klibansky, Erwin Panofsky, and Fritz Saxl, *Saturn and Melancholy: Studies in the History of Natural Philosophy, Religion and Art* (London: Thomas Nelson and Sons, Ltd., 1964), pp. 18–41.

3. See Siegfried Wenzel, *The Sin of Sloth: Acedia in Medieval Thought and Literature* (Chapel Hill: University of North Carolina Press, 1960), p. 15.

4. Kuhn, p. 39.

5. All of the following descriptive remarks are drawn from *The Praktikos*, ed. and trans. John Eudes Bamberger (Spencer, MA: Cistercian Publications, 1970), #12, pp. 18–19.

6. *Praktikos* #10, pp. 17–18. It is interesting to compare discussions on the etiological relationship between depression and anger such as those in Sigmund Freud's *Mourning and Melancholia* (1917), *Standard Edition*, vol. 14, trans. James Strachey et al. (London: Hogarth Press, 1953).

7. *Praktikos* #50, pp. 29–30.

8. Ibid., #43, p. 28.

9. For overviews of Cassian's contributions to the sins tradition, see Morton Bloomfield, *The Seven Deadly Sins* (East Lansing: Michigan State College Press, 1952), pp. 69–71; Wenzel, pp. 18–22; Kuhn, pp. 50–53. The exact composition dates of Cassian's works are disputed, but scholars estimate them as follows: *De Institutis Coenobiorum*, c. 420–424; *Collationes Patrum*, c. 426–428.

10. *Conférences*, trans. E. Pichéry (Paris: Les Editions du Cerf, 1955), V, 16; cited by Léon Christiani, *Jean Cassien: La Spiritualité du Désert* (Paris: Les Editions de Fontenelle, 1946), vol. II, p. 65. See also Wenzel, pp. 23–24 and 51. The original Latin listing of the parent sins and their progeny reads as follows: *Tristitia (rancor, amaritudo, pusillanimitas, desperatio). Acedia (otiositas, somnolentia, importunitas, curiositas, verbositas, inquietudo, pervagatio, instabilitas mentis et corporis).*

11. For passages specifying this distinction between good and evil sadness, see Cassian's *Institutions Cénobitiques*, ed. Jean-Claude Guy (Paris: Les Editions du Cerf, 1965), Section VII, 3, p. 297, and Section IX, 9–10, p. 377. Unless otherwise noted, all subsequent quoted materials are my translations into English from the French edition of Cassian's work.

12. *Institutions* IX, pp. 369, 379–381; *Conférences* V, 11, p. 201.

13. *Conférences* IV, 2, cited and trans. by Kuhn, p. 53.

14. All quoted material in this paragraph is from Cassian's *Institutes* X, 2, my translation of Christiani's French from *Jean Cassien: La Spiritualité du Désert*, vol. II, pp. 109–110.

15. *Institutes* X, 23–25, cited in Christiani, vol. II, p. 114.

16. *Conférences* V, 23, cited and trans. by Wenzel, pp. 55–56.

17. *Institutes* IX, 13, p. 379. See also Christiani, vol. II, p. 111. Cassian's repeated references to manual labor as a remedy for *acedia* indicate a tendency on his part to focus on its branch of indolence (*otiositas*). This focus narrows further as late medieval sin lists supplant the complex, internal affliction of *acedia* with the more readily visible, external sin of sloth.

18. Interestingly enough, the cardinal sins tradition after Gregory reverts to the term *acedia*, although this particular vice retains the same place in the sin sequence and by and large the same catalogue of identifying characteristics as in the Gregorian listing. The shift in terminology is likely due to a confusion fostered by the word *tristitia* between sorrow which is one of the four basic affects (in Stoic philosophy) and sadness which is sinful (in Christian tradition).

19. Gregory the Great, *Morals on the Book of Job*, pp. 490–491, referenced in Stanford Lyman, *The Seven Deadly Sins: Society and Evil* (New York: St. Martin's Press, 1978), p. 6. See also Wenzel, pp. 23–24 and 51.

20. Gregory, *Pastoral Care*, trans. Henry Davis (Westminster, MD.: The Newman Press, 1950), p. 96.

21. Søren Kierkegaard, *The Journals, A Selection*, ed. and trans. Alexander Dru (New York: Oxford University Press, 1938), p. 75.

22. Kierkegaard quotes Gregory in the original Latin, as does Dru in his edition of the *Journals*; the English translation is from Kuhn's discussion of Gregory and Kierkegaard, p. 35.

23. Kierkegaard, *Journals*, p. 76.

24. Ibid.

25. Gregory, *Pastoral Care*, p. 96.

26. For an excellent summary of the Hippocratic-Galenic humoral theory, see the chapters on "Scientific Theory of Melancholy" in Lawrence Babb, *The Elizabethan Malady: A Study of Melancholia in English Literature from 1580 to 1642* (East Lansing: Michigan State College Press, 1951), p. 96.

27. The chart is a slightly modified version of one created by W. J. Hill in the appendix to the *Summa Theologica* (New York: McGraw Hill/Blackfriars, 1967), vol. 33, p. 141.

28. Aquinas, *Summa Theologica*, trans. Eric d'Arcy (New York: McGraw Hill/Blackfriars, 1967), vol. 19, IaIIa, Q. 25, A. 2, pp. 49–51.

29. Ibid., Q. 25, A. 4, p. 55. W. J. Hill uses the terms "impulse and contending emotions" to translate concupiscible and irascible passions in an effort to harmonize Thomistic thought with more common and contemporary psychological vocabulary.

30. *Summa*, trans. J. P. Reid (New York: McGraw Hill/Blackfriars, 1965), vol. 21, IaIIae, Q. 40, A. 4, p. 13.

31. *Summa*, trans. Eric d'Arcy (New York: McGraw Hill/Blackfriars, 1975), vol. 20, Q. 37, A. 4, pp. 131–133.

32. W. J. Hill, editor's note to the *Summa*, vol. 33, Q. 20, A. 1, p. 91n. There is all the more reason to refer to this movement of aversion from something which is deemed realistically impossible by some term other than despair (such as "resignation") insofar as

despair, for Thomas, is the contrary of hope, and the object of hope must meet the criteria of being desirable, future, "arduous," and *possible*.

33. Ibid., Q. 20, A. 3, pp. 96–97n.

34. Evelyn Waugh, *The Seven Deadly Sins* (Freeport, New York: Books for Libraries Press, 1962), p. 58. I have changed the exclusive third person singular "man" language in the original to a more inclusive first person plural.

35. *Summa*, vol. 33, Q. 20, A. 3, p. 97.

36. *Summa*, trans. Thomas Gilby (New York: McGraw Hill/Black-friars, 1975), vol. 32, Q. 14, A. 2, p. 123.

37. W. J. Hill, Appendix to vol. 33 of the *Summa*, p. 175.

38. John of Wales, *Moniloquium*, Guillaume d'Auvergne, *De virtutibus*, 17, and David of Augsburg, *Formula novitiorum*, 51, all cited and trans. by Wenzel, pp. 77, 59, and 160, respectively.

39. Martin Luther, W.A. 18.719.8, cited by Susan Snyder in "The Left Hand of God: Despair in Medieval and Renaissance Tradition," *Studies in the Renaissance* XII (1965), p. 59.

40. Letter of August 2, 1527, in *Luther's Correspondence*, v. II, ed. Smith-Jacobs, cited by Vergilius Ferm in *Cross-Currents in the Personality of Martin Luther* (North Quincy, MA: The Christopher Publishing House, 1972), p. 100.

41. Cited in M. Michelet, *Life of Luther, Written by Himself, Collected and Arranged by M. Michelet*, trans. William Hazlitt (London: David Bogue, 1846), p. 208. It is significant to note here that Luther actually coins a new vocabulary to talk about "the temptations of blasphemy and despair" which he mentions here. In contrast to the word *Versuchungen*, the standard German translation for the Latin *tentatio*, he refers to the spiritual temptations of doubt, despair, blasphemy, depression and the like as *Anfechtungen*.

42. W.A. 31.1.65, Commentary on Psalm 118, cited by Warren Hovland in *"Anfechtung* in Luther's Biblical Exegesis," *Reformation Studies: Essays in Honor of Roland H. Bainton*, ed. Franklin Littell (Richmond, VA: John Knox Press, 1963), p. 65.

43. W.A. 5.169–170, cited by Gordon Rupp in *The Righteousness of God* (London: Hodder and Stoughton, 1953), p. 236.

44. W.A. 18.719.5, in Rupp, p. 282.

45. W.A. 5.176.1, in Rupp, p., 229.

46. Ibid.

47. W.A. 5.169–170, in Rupp, p. 236.

48. Tabletalk #205, in Michelet, p. 411.

49. Letter to Jonas von Stockhausen, November 27, 1532, in *Letters of Spiritual Counsel*, ed. and trans. Theodore G. Tappert (Philadelphia: Westminster Press, 1955), pp. 89–90.

50. Ibid.

51. Letter to Jerome Weller, July 1530, *Letters of Spiritual Counsel*, p. 85.

52. Tabletalk #238, in Michelet, p. 332.

53. Letter to Jerome Weller, p. 86.

54. See, e.g., Tabletalk #122, November 30, 1531, in *Tabletalk*, trans. William Hazlitt (Philadelphia: The United Lutheran Publication House, n.d.), pp. 17–18; Letter to Joachim of Anhalt, June 26, 1534, in Michelet, p. 411; Roland Bainton, *Here I Stand: A Life of Martin Luther* (New York and Nashville: Abingdon-Cokesbury Press, 1950), p. 364.

55. Bainton, p. 364.

56. Letter to Joachim of Anhalt, June 26, 1534, in Michelet, p. 411.

57. Letter to Joachim of Anhalt, May 23, 1534, in *Letters of Spiritual Counsel*, p. 93.

58. Tabletalk #522, Spring 1533, in *Tabletalk*, p. 96.

59. Tabletalk #184, in Michelet, p. 329.

60. Tabletalk #273, May 18, 1532, in *Tabletalk*, p. 37.

61. W. A. 5.385.19, *Commentary on Psalms*, in Rupp, p. 237.

62. W. A. 14.229, cited by Hovland, p. 51.

63. Bridget Gellert Lyons, *Voices of Melancholy: Studies in Literary Treatments of Melancholy in Renaissance England* (London: Routledge and Kegan Paul, 1971). Lyons suggests that the disappearance of the word *acedia* (or accidia) from English usage in the early 1500's may indicate a transfer of the traditional meanings of this concept to the newly-popular language of melancholy (see p. 163, note 18).

64. Robert Burton, *The Anatomy of Melancholy*, in 3 volumes (New York: W. J. Widdleton, 1867), Vol. I, p. 1.

65. Burton, Vol. I, p. 161.

66. Ibid., Vol. I, p. 52 (words in brackets are my translation from Burton's Latin).

67. Ibid., Vol. I, pp. 344–345.

68. Ibid., vol. III, pp. 452 and 465.

69. Ibid., Vol. III, pp. 466–467.

70. Ibid., vol. I, p. 170.

71. Ibid., vol. III, p. 456, and vol. I, pp. 332–333.

72. Ibid., vol. II, p. 52.

73. Ibid., vol. III, pp. 497–498. See also Babb, *The Elizabethan Malady*, pp. 38–39.

74. Babb, pp. 39–40, referring to Burton II, 132.

75. Burton, vol. III, p. 500.

76. Ibid., p. 501.

77. Ibid., p. 471.

78. Ibid., p. 467.

79. Ibid., p. 473.

80. Ibid.

81. Ibid., vol. I, p. 52.

82. Marquis de Laplace, cited in A. E. McKenzie, *The Major Achievements of Science* (New York: Simon and Schuster, 1960), p. 44.

83. Philip Rieff, *The Triumph of the Therapeutic: Uses of Faith After Freud* (New York: Harper and Row, 1966).

Chapter 3

1. *Oxford English Dictionary*, vol. VI (Oxford: Clarendon Press, 1933), p. 313.

2. *Either/Or*, vol. II, trans. Walter Lowrie (Princeton: Princeton University Press, 1959), pp. 199 and 193.

3. Burton, vol. I, p. 32.

4. For the etymology of the Danish and German words, I am indebted to Vincent A. McCarthy, *The Phenomenology of Moods in Kierkegaard* (Boston: Martinus Nijhoff, 1978), p. 85.

5. Søren Kierkegaard, *The Sickness Unto Death*, trans. Walter Lowrie (Princeton: Princeton University Press, 1941 and 1954), p. 164. Henceforth, page references to this work will be supplied parenthetically within the text.

6. Alvin Toffler, *Future Shock* (New York: Random House, 1970), pp. 234 ff.

7. On such issues as women's "fear of success" and preference for an ethic of responsibility and care over an ethic of rights and autonomy, see, e.g., Matina Horner, "Toward an Understanding of Achievement-Related Conflicts in Women," *Journal of Social Issues*, Vol. 28, No. 2 (1972), pp. 157–174; and Carol Gilligan, *In a Different Voice: Psychological Theory and Women's Development* (Cambridge, MA: Harvard University Press, 1982).

8. Is Kierkegaard, then, onto something in differentiating womanly from manly variants of despairing? Perhaps so in terms of societal conditioning, although I suspect not in any inherent or essentialist sense.

9. Eric Berne, *Games People Play* (New York: Grove Press, 1964 [paperback edition 1967]), pp. 115ff.

10. See chapter 2, note 54.

11. *Either/Or*, vol. II, p. 240. There is one seeming advantage to such rudimentary despair: its experience of pain is only temporary, lasting only as long as we are focusing upon our particular disappointment. However, for Kierkegaard this advantage proves nebulous, since we are actually existing in a deeper condition of despair without knowing it, and our ignorance keeps us from looking to the appropriate place for cure.

12. Kierkegaard, *Journals*, vol. I, #749, trans. Alexander Dru (London: Oxford University Press, 1938), p. 348.

13. *Purity of Heart Is to Will One Thing*, trans. Douglas Steere (New York: Harper and Brothers, 1938), p. 132.

14. Fortunately for the translator and the non-Danish reader, the English word for "despair" operates with a similar variety of following pronouns. For Kierkegaard's linguistic notes on Danish usage, see *The Sickness Unto Death*, pp. 194 and 244. His discussion of the despair of forgiveness occupies pp. 244–255; my exposition of this form of sinful despairing relies most heavily on pp. 245–246.

15. Ibid., p. 212. The quote is an allusion to Eph. 2:12, "Remember that you were at that time separated from Christ, alienated from the commonwealth of Israel, and strangers to the covenants of promise, having no hope and without God in the world."

16. *Journals*, cited in Walter Lowrie, *Kierkegaard* (London: Oxford University Press, 1938), p. 404.

17. See chapter 2, note 55.

18. See chapter 2, note 57.

Chapter 4

1. Magda Arnold and J. A. Gasson, "Feeling and Emotion as Dynamic Factors in Personality Integration," in Arnold, ed., *The Nature of Emotions* (Baltimore: Penguin Books, 1968), pp. 205ff.

2. Amélie O. Rorty, "Explaining Emotions," in Rorty, ed., *Explaining Emotions* (Berkeley: University of California Press, 1980), p. 123, n. 3.

3. Ibid., p. 117.

4. On the etiology of various forms of metabolically-induced despair, see Chapter Four, "What Causes These Disorders," in Demitri Papolos, M.D., and Janice Papolos, *Overcoming Depression* (New York: Harper and Row, 1987), pp. 55–84.

5. See Robert Solomon, *The Passions: The Myth and Nature of Human Emotion* (Notre Dame: University of Notre Dame Press, 1983), p. 172. Hereafter, page references from this work will be cited parenthetically in the text.

6. In *The Color Purple*, we see the palpability of provoking external circumstances even more vividly: the oppressions of poverty, racism, sexism, battery, and abuse are *real*, and the despair which they engender is far from being all in Celie's head. In a sense, one could even say that Celie's despair is an accurate and appropriate response to some devastating features of her situation. Yet she herself finally refuses such an assessment, recognizing that the future holds more surprises and potentials than the foreclosure of despair can foresee. Even here, then — even in the most seriously provocative of situations, despair shows itself to be bound up with a "generalizing" tendency, with beliefs or assumptions about the future course of events rather than simply with the way things are.

7. This is precisely what occurs within Celie's experience: even in the midst of radical provocations to despair, she discovers that some of her "hopes and expectations" — or, more accurately, some of her fears and non-expectations — "are the products of judgments" which she does reexamine. Recall the important passage: "Most times I feels like shit but I felt like shit before in my life and what happen? I had me a fine sister name Nettie. I had me another fine woman name Shug." (235) Thus, in light of the surprises and unexpected graces from her past, she reexamines the tempting judgment that all of her future will be as miserable as the present moment.

8. Admittedly, this tautology sounds very similar to Bainton's description of Martin Luther as prescribing faith as the cure for a lack of faith. There is, however, one significant difference: Luther's faith is a gift of grace, whereas Solomon's world is one from which grace is conspicuosly absent.

9. Robert Roberts, *Spirituality and Human Emotion* (Grand Rapids, MI: William B. Eerdmans Publishing Co., 1982), p. 96. Throughout the remainder of this section, references from this work will be given parenthetically in the text.

10. Papolos, pp. 29–30.

11. To be fair to Solomon, I must insert that he does take the existence of clinical, physiologically-induced forms of depression at least minimally into account. He writes, for example (p. 294), "I do not want to deny that depression can be 'pathological'. . . . I only want to argue that it is in itself not pathological." His quarrel is with the current "medical and antihuman Myth of the Passions" in which "depression is treated as a psychic influenza" with the prescription to "take a Librium, as you might take an aspirin for a cold." Solomon sees this "Myth" as fostering a dangerously passive attitude towards our affective experiences; through it, we come to see ourselves as victims, abdicating responsibility for the fact that our depression — or what-

ever other mood — is a strategy which we have *constructed* as a way of responding to our circumstances. The goal of Solomon's argument is to debunk the victim mentality. While I appreciate his intent, I still see times when a rigorous appeal to "self-overcoming" can do more harm than good. Sometimes the pathology of depression is so overwhelmingly strong that we really cannot help ourselves, and to tell us that we must is to push us deeper into the pit of failure and self-condemnation from which we have been struggling, so futilely and painfully, to escape. Thus, I think a more nuanced perspective on moods and their potential for "overcoming" is imperative, even given Solomon's valuable concerns that we not excuse ourselves too much.

12. Papolos, p. 139.

13. Ibid., pp. 150–151.

14. Richard R. Niebuhr, *Experiential Religion* (New York: Harper and Row, 1972), pp. 44–46.

15. Lynch, *Images of Hope*, p. 23.

Chapter 5

1. Karl Rahner and Herbert Vorgrimler, "Despair," *Dictionary of Theology*, trans. Richard Strachan, et al. (New York: Crossroads, 1981), p. 121. My emphasis.

2. This quotation and those in the following paragraph are from Waldemar Molinski, "Despair," *Sacramentum Mundi*, vol. II, ed. Karl Rahner et al. (New York: Herder and Herder, 1968), pp. 69- 70. My emphasis.

3. See Wenzel, pp. 59, 77, 160.

4. Paul Tillich, "You Are Accepted," *The Shaking of the Foundations* (New York: Charles Scribner's Sons, 1948), p. 154.

5. Paul Tillich, *The Courage to Be* (New Haven: Yale University Press, 1952), pp. 54–55. Future page references from this source will be provided parenthetically in the text.

6. Martin Luther, see chapter 2, note 62.

7. For an example of this critique, see Judith Plaskow, *Sex, Sin and Grace: Women's Experience and the Theologies of Reinhold Niebuhr and Paul Tillich* (Lanham, MD: University Press of America, 1980), p. 157.

8. See chapter 2, notes 49–57.

9. Dorothée Soelle, *Suffering*, trans. Everette R. Kalin (Philadelphia: Fortress Press, 1975), p. 107.

10. Lynch, *Images of Hope*, p. 54. Future page references from this source will be provided parenthetically in the text.

11. The approach to eschatology which I am advocating here — that of God's "wooing" the world by compassionate persuasion — is

developed in a vivid and engaging fashion in Robert Farrar Capon, *The Third Peacock: A Book About God and the Problem of Evil* (Garden City, NY: Image Books, 1972). This approach also has much in common with that of the process theologians John Cobb and David Griffin in *Process Theology: An Introductory Exposition* (Philadelphia: Westminster, 1976). Since my task here is simply to suggest what elements within the locus of Christian eschatology are most fruitful for a contemporary theological approach to understanding despair, I refer interested readers to these other sources for a more full-blown discussion of the doctrine.

12. Roberts, p. 103.

13. C. S. Lewis, *The Problem of Pain* (New York: The Macmillan Co., 1955), p. viii.

14. Kierkegaard, *The Sickness Unto Death*, p. 148.

15. For a more thorough presentation of what is entailed in a confessional theological perspective, see R. Melvin Keiser, *Recovering the Personal: Religious Language and the Post-Critical Quest of H. Richard Niebuhr* (Atlanta, GA: Scholars Press, 1988), especially pp. 126–132.

16. See as outstanding examples: Valerie Saiving [Goldstein], "The Human Situation: A Feminine View," *Journal of Religion*, 40 (April, 1960), pp. 100–112; and Judith Plaskow, *Sex, Sin and Grace*, cited earlier for its critique of Tillich's position. See note 7 above.

17. Plaskow, pp. 157ff. For a similar critique of Tillich's propensity to abstract "humanist" categories rather than concrete discussion pertinent to the struggles and experiences of women, see also Mary Daly, *Beyond God the Father* (Boston: Beacon Press, 1973), pp. 20–24 and p. 27.

18. It is always useful to look back at Paul Tillich's ethical and ontological analysis of courage in *The Courage to Be* (see note 5 above). For more on a life animated by the cardinal as well as the theological virtues, see Robert Roberts, *The Strengths of a Christian* (Philadelphia: The Westminster Press, 1984).

19. See Paul Pruyser, "Phenomenology and Dynamics of Hoping," *Journal for the Scientific Study of Religion*, vol. 3, no. 1 (Fall 1963), p. 95.

20. Tillich, *The Courage to Be*, pp. 57–63.

21. Sallie McFague, *Models of God: Theology for an Ecological, Nuclear Age* (Philadelphia: Fortress Press, 1987), p. x.

22. For a clarification of the differences between clinical and non-clinical depressions, see chapter 4, note 7.

23. Frederick Buechner, *Telling the Truth: The Gospel as Tragedy, Comedy, and Fairy Tale* (New York: Harper and Row, 1977), p. 88.